# Idaho

# IDAHO BY ROAD

NATIONAL FOREST

0 15 30 45 60 75 90
MILES

Kaniksu National Forest
Priest Lake
Sandpoint
Lake Pend Oreille
Coeur d'Alene National Forest
Coeur d'Alene
Coeur d'Alene Lake
St. Joe R.
St. Joe National Forest
St. Joe National Forest
Elk River
Moscow
Dworshak Reservoir
Clearwater National Forest
Lewiston
Snake R.
Grangeville
Selway R.
Nez Perce National Forest
Salmon R.
Warren
Payette National Forest
South Fork
Boise National Forest
Middle Fork
Salmon
Salmon National Forest
Salmon National Forest
Salmon R.
Island Park Reservoir
Targhee National Forest
Borah Peak (12,662 ft.)
Ashton
Cascade Reservoir
Snake R.
Payette R.
Weiser
Payette
Caldwell
Meridian
Boise
Nampa
Challis National Forest
Ketchum
Sawtooth National Forest
Rexburg
Targhee National Forest
Idaho Falls
Snake R.
Mountain Home
Blackfoot
Palisades Reservoir
Caribou National Forest
American Falls Reservoir
Pocatello
Blackfoot Reservoir
American Falls
Snake R.
Bruneau R.
Twin Falls
Burley
Goose Cr.
Sawtooth National Forest
Montpelier
Caribou National Forest
Cache National Forest
Bear Lake
Bear R.
Ouyhee R.

N
W E
S

# Celebrate the States

# Idaho

## Rebecca Stefoff

Marshall Cavendish
Benchmark
New York

Marshall Cavendish Benchmark
99 White Plains Road
Tarrytown, New York 10591-5502
www.marshallcavendish.us

All Internet sites were correct at time of printing.

Library of Congress Cataloging-in-Publication Data
Stefoff, Rebecca
Idaho / by Rebecca Stefoff.—2nd ed.
p. cm. — (Celebrate the states)
Summary: "Provides comprehensive information on the geography, history, wildlife, governmental
structure, economy, cultural diversity, peoples, religion, and landmarks of
Idaho"—Provided by publisher.
Includes bibliographical references and index.
ISBN-978-0-7614-3003-2
1. Idaho—Juvenile literature. I. Title.
F746.3.S74 2008
979.6—dc22
2007029496

Editor: Christine Florie
Contributing Editor: Nikki Bruno Clapper
Publisher: Michelle Bisson
Art Director: Anahid Hamparian
Series Designer: Adam Mietlowski

Photo research by Connie Gardner

Cover photo by David Muench/CORBIS

The photographs in this book are used by permission and through the courtesy of: *Idaho Stock Images:*
Steve Smith, 8; Milan Chuckovich, 16; William H. Mullins, 18, 101, 103; Glenn Oakley, 61, 98; Steve
Bly, 63; Chad Chase, 64; Marjorie McBride, 66; Quicksilver Studios, 76; Marc Auth, 97; Patrick Stoll,
back cover; *Image Works:* Andre Jenny, 11; Michael Wickes, 14, 90; David Frazier, 15, 32, 60, 81, 105
(B), 132; Topham, 38, 45; Stephen Jaffe, 52; Joe Sohm, 68; Roger Viollet, 121; *Danita Delimont:* 13,
27, 95; *NativeStock:* Marilyn "Angel" Wynn, 31, 33, 59, 118; *Corbis:* George D. Lepp, 19; Jim
Richardson, 23; David Frazier, 25; Marilyn "Angel" Wynn,/NativeStock, 28; James L. Amos, 34;
Bettmann, 36, 47, 49 (T), 49 (B), 50, 123, 130; Arthur Rothstein, 48; David Stocklein, 54; Karl
Weatherly, 62, 88; Stephen Sherbill, 70; Vince Streano, 78; Becky Luigart-Stayner, 83; Kevin R. Morris,
86, 93, 102, 117; Michael T. Sedam, 99; Scott Smith, 100; Neil Rabinowitz, 114; John Springer
Collection, 125; Wally McNamee, 127, 129; Michael S. Lewis, 135; David Muench, 137; *Getty Images:*
Jim and Janie Dutcher, 21; Hulton Archive, 41; Neal Mishler, 105 (T); *Minden Pictures:* Michael
Quinton, 26; Konrad Wothe, 109; *AP Photo:* 71; *NorthWind Picture Archives:* 39 (T), 39 (B).

Printed in Malaysia
1 3 5 6 4 2

# Contents

Idaho Is . . .                                                           6

**Chapter One**                                                          9
**Geography:** Snow and Sagebrush
The Shape of the Land ▪ Winter and Summer ▪ Wild Idaho ▪ Endangered
Plants and Animals ▪ Using Land and Water

**Chapter Two**                                                          29
**History:** Inventing Idaho
Idaho's First People ▪ Native Cultures ▪ From Exploration to Settlement ▪
Toward Statehood ▪ The Twentieth Century and Beyond

**Chapter Three**                                                        55
**People:** North, South—and West
A State with Three Capitals ▪ Ethnic Idaho ▪ Recreation and Culture ▪
An American Paradise?

**Chapter Four**                                                         69
**Government:** Making Decisions
The Executive Branch ▪ The Legislature ▪ The Judicial System ▪ Fighting
for Control

**Chapter Five**                                                         79
**Economy:** Growing Industries
Agriculture: Potatoes and More ▪ Timber and Mining ▪ Trading Across the
Border ▪ Catching the Tourist Dollar

**Chapter Six**                                                          91
**Landmarks:** Gem State Road Trip
Northern Idaho ▪ Central Idaho ▪ Southern Idaho

**State Survey**                                                         105

**Find Out More**                                                        138

**Index**                                                               141

# Idaho Is . . .

## Idaho is something of a mystery to many Americans . . .

"Idaho remains one of the least known and most puzzling of American states. It is the 'riddle of the Rockies' to many out-of-state commentators."

—historian Carlos A. Schwantes, *In Mountain Shadows: A History of Idaho*, 1991

"Because it is stuck between the open land of Washington and Oregon and the Continental Divide of the Rockies, Idaho gets left out. Is it Rocky Mountain country? Perhaps. Is it the Northwest? Perhaps. Is it anything, but Idaho?"

—writer Sallie Tisdale, *Stepping Westward*, 1991

## . . . and life there can be challenging . . .

"In the raw new land of South Idaho it was shove and scrape, and if you had bad luck or lost your strength you were done for."

—Nancy Stringfellow, describing her 1920s childhood near Twin Falls

"What the state needs to realize is that there aren't enough jobs out there and people who have good jobs are paying for the ones who don't. I think if we had more jobs then the poverty rate in Idaho would drop significantly."

—student essay on young-adult poverty in Idaho, Partners for Prosperity, www.easternidahoprosperity.org

"At first I pretty much hated it here. I missed the city, skate parks and having a lot of things to do. But I got used to it, and now I like Idaho. There's a lot to do here, it's just different from the city. My friends in Seattle think I'm on permanent vacation."

—Joey Sanroman, whose family moved from Seattle to Idaho when he was fourteen

**. . . but people treasure the beauty of life in Idaho—or dream of living there.**

"In my heart, I can still see tribal people canoeing up and down the lake. They're singing songs."
—Richard Mullen, Coeur d'Alene Tribal Council member

"A lovely, level country spread out for miles and the broad expanse of water lay as a front view, with tall mountains beyond it."
—Martha Gay Masterson, early settler near Lake Coeur d'Alene

"Compared to my own bulging, booming state of Arizona, the future of Idaho looks clean, bright, free and hopeful. Maybe I'll move."
—environmentalist and author Edward Abbey, 1985

*Idaho is a state with an identity crisis. Formed from leftover pieces of other territories, it seems to lack a definite identity of its own. Even its name—a fake "Indian" word—was originally meant for another state. Geography divides Idaho into two distinct regions, and some Idahoans find it easier to identify with their neighbors in nearby states than with the rest of their own state. Divided and ruggedly independent as they are, however, Idahoans are united in the proud affection they feel for their state. They are torn between wanting to sing its praises and wanting to keep its secrets to themselves.*

## Chapter One

# Snow and Sagebrush

"A quirky place" is how one young woman describes her home state of Idaho. She grew up in the sun-baked southwestern corner of the state, in a region of rolling hills and broad grasslands. Now she lives in Sandpoint, a growing town in Idaho's forested, mountainous northern panhandle. "Idaho's got all kinds of people, just like it's got all kinds of weather," she says.

Idaho is a bit of almost everything the West has to offer. It is bounded on the west by the Pacific Northwest states of Washington and Oregon. To the south are the high desert states of Nevada and Utah. On the east are the mountain states of Wyoming and Montana. The Continental Divide—the high, winding track through the Rocky Mountains that separates North America's east-flowing rivers from its west-flowing ones—forms part of Idaho's eastern border. North of Idaho is the Canadian province of British Columbia.

*Sagebrush, lush and green from the spring rains, covers the fields and hillsides that rise toward the Sawtooth Mountains.*

# LAND AND WATER

| | |
|---|---|
| | > 10,000 ft. |
| | 6,000 – 10,000 ft. |
| | 3,000 – 6,000 ft. |
| | 1,500 – 3,000 ft. |
| | 600 – 1,500 ft. |

0   15   30   45   60   75   90

MILES

*Kaniksu National Forest*

*Priest Lake*

Sandpoint

*Lake Pend Oreille*

*Coeur d'Alene National Forest*

Coeur d'Alene

*Coeur d'Alene Lake*

*St. Joe R.*

*St. Joe National Forest*

*St. Joe National Forest*

Elk River

Moscow

*Dworshak Reservoir*

*Clearwater National Forest*

Lewiston

*Snake R.*

*Selway R.*

Grangeville

*Nez Perce National Forest*

N
W    E
S

*Salmon R.*

Warren

*Payette National Forest*

Salmon

*South Fork*

*Salmon National Forest*

*Boise National Forest*

*Middle Fork*

*Salmon R.*

*Salmon National Forest*

*Cascade Reservoir*

*Island Park Reservoir*

*Targhee National Forest*

Weiser

*Payette R.*

▲ *Borah Peak (12,662 ft.)*

Ashton

Payette

Rexburg

Caldwell

Meridian

Ketchum

*Challis National Forest*

*Targhee National Forest*

Boise

*Sawtooth National Forest*

Nampa

Idaho Falls

*Snake R.*

*Palisades Reservoir*

Blackfoot

*Caribou National Forest*

Mountain Home

*Snake R.*

*American Falls Reservoir*

Pocatello

American Falls

*Blackfoot Reservoir*

*Bear R.*

*Bruneau R.*

Twin Falls

Burley

Montpelier

*Goose Cr.*

*Caribou National Forest*

*Cache National Forest*

*Owyhee R.*

*Sawtooth National Forest*

*Bear Lake*

## THE SHAPE OF THE LAND

Idaho's shape has been described as a hatchet, a pork chop, and a pregnant letter L. The state's narrow northern section, called the panhandle, is only 45 miles wide at the Canadian border. Idaho is widest at its southern border, which measures 316 miles from east to west. Between these borders is the nation's thirteenth-largest state, almost 84,000 square miles of extremely varied terrain.

The swift-flowing Salmon River is called the River of No Return because its speed and rapids prevent canoeists from paddling upstream. The Salmon flows from east to west across the middle of Idaho. Surrounded by steep, tumbled mountain ranges, it divides Idaho into two regions, north and south. Except for a few plateaus, prairies, and meadows, most of Idaho is a great sea of mountains. On a road map, a great many highways and byways in Idaho are labeled SCENIC DRIVE. It is the twists, turns, and sudden dramatic vistas of the mountain landscape that make so many roads scenic.

Of Idaho's eighty or so mountain ranges, two of the

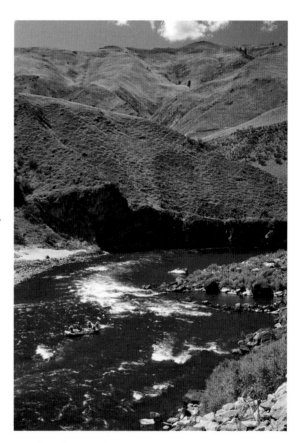

*Rafters brave the rapids on the Salmon River, also called the River of No Return.*

most forbidding are the Bitterroot Range of the Rockies along the eastern border and the jagged Sawtooth Mountains in south-central Idaho. The Selkirk and Coeur d'Alene ranges dominate the panhandle. Mount Borah, Idaho's highest peak at 12,662 feet, rises from the Lost River Range east of the Sawtooths. The Seven Devils Mountains guard Idaho's western border with Oregon. The Grand Tetons—called by one English traveler in the 1880s "the most perfect example in the world of how mountains should appear on the horizon"—march along its eastern border with Wyoming. The state's southeastern corner contains the Caribou Mountains and the Blue Spring Hills.

Between the clustered peaks of south-central Idaho and the southeastern highlands is the Snake River Plain. The Snake River begins in a spring in Wyoming. It enters Idaho and flows west across the southern part of the state in a long, lazy arc. At the Oregon border the Snake plunges into a gorge called Hells Canyon—the deepest river gorge in North America—before joining the Columbia River, which eventually empties into the Pacific Ocean.

The Snake River Plain is the flattest part of Idaho. Over thousands of years the river has carved a deep canyon through the heart of the plain. In most places the water now flows at the foot of steep canyon walls or cliffs. Above the river, on the level plain, occasional isolated hills or steep rocky buttes break up the flat landscape.

The southwestern corner of Idaho, far from the river, is much like the neighboring areas of Nevada, Utah, and southeastern Oregon—a high-altitude desert of dry, rolling hills and canyons carved by creeks that often dry up in summer. Rancher Dave Amberson, who grew up in this sternly beautiful part of the state, calls it "a hard place to love, but hard to get out of your blood."

*Idaho's flattest landscapes and most fertile farmland are found on the Snake River Plain, which forms the southern part of the state.*

## WINTER AND SUMMER

The mountains of central Idaho divide the state into two climate zones. Northern Idaho has a climate like that of Washington and Oregon. Winters are wet and cold, summers warm and dry. Parts of the panhandle receive 96 inches of rain and snow a year—nearly as much as Washington's Olympic Peninsula, one of the nation's wettest places.

Southern Idaho's climate is like that of the Rocky Mountain and Great Plains states. Winters are cold and windy but drier than those farther north, while summers are hot and dry. Fierce summer thunderstorms sometimes rumble across the plains. Lightning stabs down at the parched land from towering black clouds and ignites wildfires.

"Weather forecasting? Well, that's tricky," admits a park ranger in central Idaho. "Mountains make their own weather systems, and the weather can change in an instant. We get all kinds of extremes. You can be hiking on a hot July day and get caught in a hailstorm—or a snowstorm." Snow and ice can bring travel to a standstill, especially in central Idaho. Remember those roads marked SCENIC DRIVE? Many of them are also marked MAY BE CLOSED IN WINTER.

Snow is vital to Idaho's well-being, however. It not only thrills skiers but also provides snowmelt to feed the Selway, Lochsa, Clearwater, Coeur d'Alene, Big Lost, and Salmon rivers, as well as hundreds of smaller waterways. Snowmelt also waters Idaho's forests and replenishes its more than two thousand lakes.

*A snowboarder gazes toward the Grand Teton Mountains, which straddle the border at Targhee Ski Resort.*

Summer often brings trouble to the West in the form of wildfires. Fire season gets under way when lightning—or human carelessness—causes wildfires to start. Dry weather and high winds help the fires spread. In 2000, Idaho experienced one of the worst fire seasons in its history. More than 559,000 acres burned in several national forests and other public lands. Just three years earlier, however, Idaho had received unusually heavy rainfall and snowfall. The extra water had flooded the drainage basins of the Weiser and Payette rivers in the southwestern part of the state.

*A wildfire rages in Boise National Forest. Like other western states, Idaho is at risk of wildfires when lightning—or human carelessness—ignites dry summer forests.*

Nearly two-fifths of Idaho's land is forested. Again, there is a big difference between the regions north and south of the Salmon River. More than 80 percent of northern Idaho is covered with forest, compared with less than 30 percent in the south. Evergreens such as Douglas fir, western white pine, and western red cedar flourish in the moist, cool hills and mountains north of the Snake River Plain. The drier south is sagebrush country, an open landscape covered with hardy grasses and shrubs that can withstand heat, cold, and drought. Streams and creeks are lined with stands of birch, aspen, willow, and cottonwood trees whose leaves blaze golden in the fall.

Huge herds of bison once roamed across southern Idaho. Today there are only a few of these shaggy beasts left, mostly on private and tribal ranchland. Grizzly bears, black bears, cougars, mountain goats, and bighorn sheep are also less numerous than they once were, but enough of these animals remain to make Idaho a wildlife watcher's paradise. There are also moose, elk, white-tailed deer, pronghorn antelope, beavers, porcupines, wolverines, and prairie dogs. Rock-strewn mountain slopes echo to the whistles of

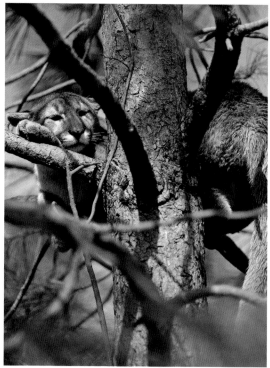

*A cougar, North America's largest wild cat, rests in a tree.*

groundhog-like marmots and the shrill "meep, meep" calls of pikas—small, shy, rabbitlike creatures that dwell among boulders.

More than 350 species of birds have been seen in Idaho. Some live there year-round, while others pass through as they migrate. Waterbirds such as herons, geese, and ducks are plentiful around lakes and rivers. Smaller species that live in meadows and prairies include hummingbirds, meadowlarks, and the mountain bluebird, Idaho's state bird.

Idaho is especially rich in birds of prey—hawks, falcons, and eagles. The Snake River Birds of Prey Natural Area near the town of Kuna in southern Idaho has the nation's largest concentration of these birds. They nest in the rocky canyon walls and soar on widespread wings to scan Idaho's rugged landscape with their keen hunters' eyes.

### ENDANGERED PLANTS AND ANIMALS

Like other states, Idaho has its share of endangered species. Under the Endangered Species Act of 1973, the U.S. Fish and Wildlife Service (USFWS) maintains a list of species that it has identified as endangered or threatened. Endangered species are at high risk of becoming extinct in most or all of their habitats. Threatened species are likely to become endangered. As of 2007, the USFWS recognized twenty-four threatened and endangered species in Idaho.

Four of the threatened species are plants. They are Spalding's catch-fly, Ute ladies'-tresses, water howellia, and Macfarlane's four-o'clock. Spalding's catch-fly was added to the list most recently, in 2001. There are two bird species on the list. The Eskimo curlew is endangered. The bald eagle is listed as threatened, but it will most likely be taken off the list because its populations have made a comeback in many parts of the United States.

*Macfarlane's four-o'clock is a rare and federally protected wildflower that grows along river-banks. In Idaho it is found in several places, including some hillsides in Hells Canyon.*

The grizzly bear, woodland caribou, Canada lynx, and gray wolf are the largest and most recognizable of Idaho's endangered animals. Much smaller, but still in peril, are the pygmy Columbia Basin rabbit and the northern Idaho ground squirrel. Six fish species, including salmon, trout, and sturgeon, are considered endangered or threatened. Six smaller creatures, mostly snails, are in danger of becoming extinct.

Many of Idaho's citizens contribute their time and money to protecting the state's endangered plants and animals. They support organizations such as the Idaho Wildlife Federation (IWF), which seeks to preserve the habitat of a bird called the sage grouse. The sage grouse isn't on the list of endangered species, but it is moving in that direction. The goal of the IWF and other conservation groups is to keep the sage grouse off the list by restoring and protecting the areas where the bird raises its young.

Endangered species are a concern to the state's government, too. In 2000, state officials established the Governor's Office of Species Conservation (OSC). Its purpose is to bring together conservation organizations, wildlife management agencies, biologists, and business interests that have a stake in how Idaho approaches the safeguarding of its species. One of the OCS's roles is to develop protection plans with landowners who have endangered species on their properties. These plans are meant to balance the needs of protected species with the rights and needs of landowners and the economic development of the state.

One example of the OSC's approach to conservation involves the southern Idaho ground squirrel. This species is not yet listed under the Endangered Species Act, but it is a candidate for listing in the future. If the squirrel makes the list, federal regulations would begin governing land use where the squirrel lives, in Idaho's Weiser River Basin. OSC leaders hope to keep the squirrel off the list by keeping its numbers from falling too sharply.

Most southern Idaho ground squirrels live on private property. The OSC offers property owners Candidate Conservation Agreements with Assurances, or CCAAs.

*Smaller than other ground squirrels, the northern Idaho ground squirrel is an endangered species clinging to its existence.*

Under these agreements, landowners promise to use conservation practices that will limit the threats to the squirrels. In return, the USFWS promises landowners that if the southern Idaho ground squirrel does become a listed species under the Endangered Species Act, the landowners will not have to submit to additional conservation rules. It is too soon to tell whether the IOC's strategy is working.

The controversy surrounding another species shows how difficult it can be to balance different points of view about wildlife conservation. To many people, the gray wolf embodies the spirit of the American wilderness. To others, however, the wolf is a livestock-killing nuisance. Once almost wiped out throughout the West, the gray wolf was listed as an endangered species in 1985. Ten years later, the USFWS began to reintroduce wolves into Idaho's federal lands, such as wilderness areas. By 2006, according to the OSC, the state had about 650 wolves in some 70 packs.

Idaho's wolf-recovery plan was more successful than expected. State officials asked the USFWS to take the wolf off Idaho's Endangered Species list. The USFWS turned over some wolf-management responsibilities to the state. Then, in early 2007, it proposed removing the gray wolf from the list in Idaho. The wolf will remain on the list, however, until the "de-listing" process is final. That may take some time, because conservation groups have vowed to fight the de-listing, in court if necessary. They fear that once wolves are removed from the protection of the Endangered Species Act, people will once again shoot and trap them into extinction.

Many wildlife supporters argue that the threat to wolves is immediate. As soon as Idaho received some responsibility for wolf management, reports the Defenders of Wildlife Action Fund, "state officials announced plans to kill as many as fifty wolves in the state's Upper Clearwater Basin—75 percent of the wolf population in one National Forest. Now Idaho has asked for permission to kill wolves in areas of Northern Idaho where they are still protected under the Endangered Species Act." Idaho has had one of the nation's most successful wolf-reintroduction programs, but the final fate of its wolves remains unknown.

*Magnificent symbol of the wilderness or destroyer of livestock? The gray wolf is the subject of heated debates among Idahoans.*

## THE FATE OF THE WILDERNESS

The federal government owns 64 percent of Idaho's land. Much of this land consists of eleven national forests. Within central Idaho's national forests are 4 million acres of land set aside as wilderness areas under federal protection. These areas are called the Selway-Bitterroot Wilderness, the Frank Church River of No Return Wilderness, the Gospel Hump Wilderness, and the Sawtooth Wilderness.

Unlike most national forests, wilderness areas are protected from activities such as road building, logging, and mining. Conservationists argue that such protection is necessary to preserve Idaho's natural heritage, for the health of the land and for the enjoyment of future generations. Many Idahoans disagree with the conservationist viewpoint, however. In a state where large numbers of people have traditionally made their living from industries such as logging and mining, many citizens feel that locking up large tracts of backcountry land costs the state jobs and money.

In 1989, Steve Symms, a U.S. senator from Idaho, called the wilderness issue "a political hot potato"—something extremely difficult to handle. That is still true. The conflict between those who want to save Idaho's wilderness and those who want to use it is one of the core issues of political life in Idaho.

## USING LAND AND WATER

Much of Idaho is too mountainous for farming. The Snake River Plain, however, is flat and covered with fertile volcanic soil. Without the help of the Snake River, which provides a constant supply of water for irrigation, this land would be much too dry for agriculture. Of the total irrigated farmland in the United States, nearly one-tenth is in Idaho.

The Snake River Plain's level land and steady water supply have made it Idaho's center of settlement and urban growth. Two-thirds of Idahoans live within 50 miles of the Snake's banks. The state's five largest cities—Boise, Pocatello, Idaho Falls, Nampa, and Meridian—are located on or near the river. In contrast, some counties in central Idaho have less than one person per square mile.

*Irrigation is the key to Idaho's good harvests. Rainfall can be sparse, so farmers depend on water drawn from rivers and reservoirs.*

People have changed the face of Idaho, especially in the south, where plowed fields, orchards, and the fence lines of ranches draw straight lines across the rolling landscape. Above all, people have changed the rivers. Once the Snake River's 570-mile course through Idaho was a series of turbulent waterfalls and churning rapids. The mighty Snake dropped more than 6,000 feet from its source high in the mountains to where it meets the Columbia. Today several dozen dams tame the river's flow and turn long stretches of it into sluggish, slow-moving reservoirs.

The Snake's dams have played a vital role in Idaho's development. They provide water for irrigation and hydroelectric power for industries and homes. Progress always comes at a price, however, and in Idaho it is salmon that have paid the price. Once Idaho's rivers teemed with these fish, which spend part of their lives in the ocean but migrate far up freshwater streams to breed. Each new dam made it harder for salmon to struggle upstream to their spawning grounds and to swim downstream to the sea. Today there are few salmon in Idaho rivers—even in the Salmon River.

The U.S. Army Corps of Engineers owns and operates four dams on the lower Snake River. In the late 1990s, the corps announced that it was studying the possibility of removing the dams to increase the number of salmon that make it to Idaho. In the city of Lewiston on the Snake River, people became outraged. Many people claim that the local economy depends on cheap electricity and river shipping. Without the dams these sources of income would disappear. A port official in Lewiston called the idea of eliminating the dams "crazy" and "out of left field." Between 1984 and 1998, government agencies in the Snake River region spent $3 billion on fish ladders, hatcheries, and other programs to improve conditions for the salmon—without success.

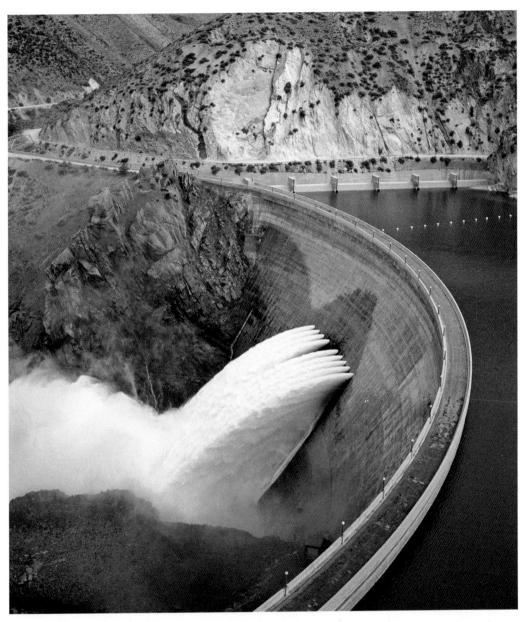

*Dams along Idaho's rivers provide electricity and water for irrigation, but they also interfere with the migration routes of Pacific Northwest salmon. In this picture, water pours through Arrowrock Dam on the Boise River.*

Since 2000, the OSC has been working with federal agencies, as well as state agencies in Washington, Oregon, and Montana, to plan for the protection and recovery of salmon populations in the rivers of the Northwest. Even with strict limits on salmon fishing and federal enforcement of water-use laws, however, the fish populations have not rebounded. The plight of the salmon shows that there are no easy answers to Idaho's environmental problems.

Pollution has also been a problem for Idahoans. Silver Valley, the valley of the Coeur d'Alene River in northern Idaho, is the largest silver-producing area in the world. It is also a dangerously polluted region. In the mid-1980s, the sparkling blue waters of Lake Coeur d'Alene were found to be contaminated with one of the highest levels of lead in the United States. The lead, along with other dangerous materials, had flowed downstream for years from mining operations on the Coeur d'Alene River.

*Kokanee salmon spawn in an Idaho stream. When this species is found in the ocean, it is called sockeye salmon.*

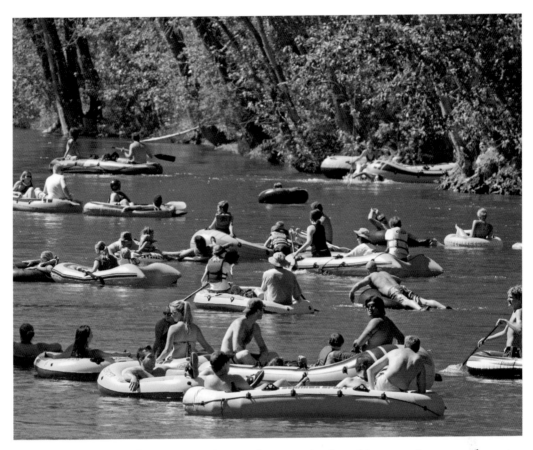

*The formerly polluted Boise River has made a comeback and is an environmental success story for Idaho.*

Idaho has made great strides toward reducing pollution, largely because of stricter laws limiting the amount of harmful substances that businesses can discharge into the air and water. The Boise River, once badly damaged by waste from sawmills and meatpacking plants, is now so clean that people can safely float down it on a raft. Many polluted sites remain, however. Idahoans must stay alert if they are to protect their land, air, and water from new sources of pollution.

## Chapter Two

# Inventing Idaho

Idaho is new. Of the lands that would become the fifty United States, Idaho was the last to be explored by people of European descent. It did not become a state until 1890. But Idaho's human history stretches far into the past and weaves together the stories of many different kinds of people.

## IDAHO'S FIRST PEOPLE

People first appeared in Idaho about 12,000 years ago—perhaps even earlier. They descended from wandering hunters who had crossed into present-day Alaska from Asia and then spread out across North America. We know about these ancient people only through a few remains, such as scattered bones and traces of old hunting camps. They were the ancestors of the Native Americans who have lived in Idaho for thousands of years.

Idaho became home to seven Native-American groups. The Kutenai, Coeur d'Alene, and Kalispell peoples lived in northern Idaho. North-central Idaho, along with parts of eastern Washingon and Oregon, formed the homeland of the Nez Perce. Some Palouse people lived along the western

*Randy'L Teton, who was the model for the image of Sacajawea on the U.S. dollar coin, is a member of the Shoshone people, one of the Native-American nations of Idaho.*

edge of central Idaho, next to the Nez Perce. The Shoshone lived across the high desert sagebrush country of southern Idaho. Mingled with the Shoshone were a closely related group called the Bannock. Another related group, the Northern Paiute, lived in the southwestern corner of Idaho and in southeastern Oregon.

## NATIVE CULTURES

Anthropologists—scholars who study the peoples of the world and their societies—have divided the Native Americans of North America into a number of large culture areas. Each of these culture areas contains a number of tribes, or peoples, whose cultures are similar in important ways. Their languages might be closely related, or they might share the same beliefs, legends, and customs. Some tribes within the same culture area have fought each other in wars, but they also have traded, intermarried, and lived in similar ways.

Idaho is part of two of these large culture areas, the Plateau and the Great Basin. Tribes from other culture areas influenced some of Idaho's native tribes. For example, both the Nez Perce and the Shoshone acquired horses, hunting methods, and even clothing styles from Great Plains tribes such as the Blackfoot and the Sioux.

### Plateau Peoples

Idaho's Kutenai, Kalispell, Coeur d'Alene, Palouse, and Nez Perce tribes share the Plateau culture. The resources of northern Idaho's rivers and forests shaped the traditional lives of these peoples.

Although the Plateau Indians usually lived in settled, permanent villages with between thirty and two hundred inhabitants, they also moved with the seasons to temporary hunting or harvesting camps. At certain times of the year, when salmon swam upriver in great numbers to

*The Looking Glass band of the Nez Perce made this longhouse to celebrate seasonal rituals called the First Fruits and First Salmon Rites.*

spawn, people from many villages would gather along riverbanks at good fishing spots, such as the sides of rapids or waterfalls. Using hooks, traps, spears, and nets, the men would catch as many fish as possible. The women would preserve the catch by drying the fish in the sun or in smoke, so that they could be eaten throughout the coming year. Men also hunted for small game such as marmots, squirrels, and rabbits, as well as big game such as deer, elk, and bear. Many hunts were group activities. Men worked together to encircle animals with a ring of fire or to drive them into a lake so that they would be easier targets.

Plateau women had their own food-gathering calendar. In spring and fall they collected wild berries. Huckleberries, which ripen in many mountainous areas in the fall, were especially important. In June and July, the women used specially prepared sticks to dig up another key part of the Plateau diet: roots such as wild carrot, onion, and camas (a type of lily with an edible root). During this root-gathering season, large groups of Native Americans would gather at harvesting grounds. They met to trade goods and to hold social events such as marriages.

The Nez Perce acquired horses in the early 1700s. They quickly became skilled riders, and they traveled to the Great Plains to hunt and to trade. The Nez Perce borrowed some customs, such as making buffalo-skin tepees, from the Plains Indians. In the rolling, hilly district called the Palouse, in northwestern Idaho and eastern Washington, the Nez Perce and Palouse Indians bred a type of strong, spotted horse now known as an Appaloosa.

*An Appaloosa mare nurses her colt. Native peoples in Idaho and Washington developed the Appaloosa breed.*

## Great Basin Peoples

Archaeologists—scientists who study the remains of cultures—think that the Shoshone and the Bannock people came from the Southwest, the area that is now Arizona and New Mexico. Thousands of years ago these tribes began migrating to Mexico, California, Nevada, and Utah. About four thousand years ago, they reached southern Idaho.

The Native Americans of the Great Basin culture area were highly skilled at surviving in challenging environments, including deserts. For example, the Northern Paiute occupied arid territory, where big game was extremely rare, but they scoured the land for pine nuts, birds, and small game such as rabbits. In addition to small game, the Shoshone-Bannock, who ranged over a much larger part of Idaho, hunted pronghorn antelope, bison, deer, and bighorn sheep. Their weapons included traps, spears, and—beginning about 1,500 years ago—bows and arrows.

*The Shoshone were highly skilled at hunting on horseback. They sometimes killed bison by driving them over cliffs.*

Among the Great Basin groups, women did the fishing. They placed traps woven of sticks and plant fibers in streams to catch fish. The women also gathered berries, pine nuts, and the seeds of wild grasses such as Nevada bluegrass. They ground the seeds into powder and stored it for the winter.

Instead of building permanent settlements, most Great Basin Indians lived a nomadic life. They moved around in family groups or small bands in search of fresh food. These bands could usually be found in the valleys during the winter. They went up into the more exposed highlands during the summer. Often larger groups gathered at fishing spots or winter camps.

Around 1700, the Shoshone obtained horses from other Native Americans. Horses allowed them to travel east to the Great Plains to hunt bison and to trade with other tribes, which were beginning to acquire European trade items. The Shoshone was one of the last tribes in the region to own firearms, however. Their neighbors to the east and south—the Arapaho, Blackfoot, Cheyenne, and Ute Indians—obtained guns and began attacking the Shoshone in an attempt to drive them back into the mountains of Idaho.

The Shoshone also went to war with the Nez Perce from time to time, but the tribes usually stopped fighting in summertime. They even did business with one another at the annual Native-American rendezvous. This gathering of many tribes took place each year near the site of the present-day town of Weiser, Idaho. For a month or two Native Americans from all directions traded, gambled, and danced together peacefully. The rendezvous, which continued into the 1860s, was a major event in the lives of the Idaho Indians.

*A powwow at Fort Hall is an occasion for wearing traditional Shoshone-Bannock clothing.*

## IRON-MAN: A SHOSHONE TALE

This Shoshone story shows how some Native Americans wove the newly arrived Euro-Americans into their tales and legends:

Iron-Man, the father of the white people, lived on the water. Wolf, the father of the Native Americans, lived underground. One day Iron-Man invited Wolf to visit. Iron-Man gave his pipe to Wolf, who smoked up all of the tobacco. Then the father of the Native Americans took his little pipe from his quiver and handed it to Iron-Man. The father of the white men smoked until the house was full of smoke, but he could not smoke up all of the tobacco in the pipe. Wolf's son told his father that Iron-Man was nearly dead, so Wolf made the smoke disappear and made Iron-Man well again. Then Iron-Man brought a large iron ball and gave half to his friend. "We are now going to make guns," he said. Both made guns as quickly as possible. Wolf made more guns in the same time than Iron-Man. That is how the father of the Native Americans won that contest.

In this tale, the Native Americans defeated the whites in a contest involving guns. Perhaps it reveals the Native Americans' wish that they *could* make guns, for in the end they lost the biggest contest of all to the force of the whites.

## FROM EXPLORATION TO SETTLEMENT

The first European Americans to arrive in Idaho were explorers on a mission for the United States. Some of those who followed came in search of furs, and some came to preach and to teach. It was many years, however, before the first settlers came to Idaho to stay.

### The Explorers

From May 1804 to September 1806, Meriwether Lewis and William Clark led a small expedition called the Corps of Discovery west from St. Louis on the Missouri River to the mouth of the Columbia River on the Pacific Ocean—and back again. They were the first white Americans to cross the West. Although they encountered many hardships during the journey, crossing Idaho was the worst part.

*Sacajawea accompanied explorers Meriwether Lewis and William Clark on their journey across North America, including a difficult crossing of Idaho. Her ability to communicate with Shoshone along the way helped make the expedition a success.*

In August 1805, the Lewis and Clark expedition crossed the Continental Divide at Lemhi Pass and stood at the edge of Idaho. Ahead of them stretched a wilderness of savage peaks, a landscape too difficult to cross. They struggled north to Lolo Pass and tried again to head west, only to become lost and snowbound in what expedition member Patrick Gass called "this horrible mountainous desert." Food was in such short supply that they dined on bear oil and candles. Finally they made contact with friendly Nez Perce, who fed the explorers and guided the expedition out of the Bitterroot Mountains. When Lewis and Clark returned to St. Louis the following year, they spoke enthusiastically of the wonders of the West, but they had little good to say about the tortuous terrain and difficult conditions of what would become Idaho.

### Mountain Men and Missionaries

Europe's passion for fur hats and coats sent trappers and traders far into the American West in search of beaver pelts. Soon after the return of the Corps of Discovery, a Canada-based British firm called the North West Company sent agent David Thompson to set up a fur trade in the region Lewis and Clark had explored. In 1809, Thompson established a trading post called Kullyspell House on the shores of Lake Pend Oreille. His post, the first non-Indian structure in Idaho, lasted for about two years. Beginning in 1818, British trappers from Canada descended into Idaho each year in what were called the Snake River brigades. The brigades reaped thousands of valuable beaver pelts, but hostile Native Americans and rough terrain made the ventures so dangerous that one trapper vowed he would return only when the beaver had skins of gold.

The Americans were not about to let the British get all the furs in the northern Rockies. Andrew Henry of St. Louis led a party of American trappers into Idaho in 1810. Gradually, more American trappers trekked into the area. These hardy adventurers were called mountain men. Some of them, including Jim Bridger and John Colter, were among the foremost explorers of the western mountains. Between 1825 and 1840, mountain men met each summer at a rowdy gathering to drink, to gamble, and to sell their furs to traders from back east. One such trader, Nathaniel Wyeth of Boston, founded a permanent trading post near present-day Pocatello in 1834. He named it Fort Hall, and it became a major outpost in the Snake River country.

*Jim Bridger was one of the fur-hunting mountain men of the Rockies.*

The glory days of the fur trade were over by 1850. By then a new wave of outsiders had begun coming to Idaho, not to hunt beaver but to guide the Native Americans toward Christianity and Euro-American civilization.

The first Protestant missionaries to enter Idaho were Henry and Eliza Spalding, who traveled west in 1836 with another missionary couple, the Whitmans. The Whitmans established a mission in eastern Washington State, while the Spaldings set themselves up at Lapwai in western Idaho. A few years later another missionary couple established a mission near Kamiah. These missions were hastily abandoned after a tragic incident in which Native Americans, angered by an outbreak of disease introduced by white newcomers, killed the Whitmans and other whites in Washington. This first Protestant missionary effort accomplished little in its eleven-year existence. Only twenty-one Native Americans converted to Christianity.

The Roman Catholic Church also sent missionaries into Idaho and the Pacific Northwest. One of the first, Pierre Jean De Smet, founded a mission among the Coeur d'Alene Indians. The Catholics proved more successful than the Protestants had been. Within a few generations, two-thirds of the Coeur d'Alene tribe had joined the Catholic Church. The Sacred Heart Mission in Cataldo, a church built in the late 1840s by Catholic missionaries and their converts, is the oldest surviving building in Idaho.

### Pioneers and Settlers

The mountain men and the missionaries opened the way for overland travel across the northern Rockies. Land-hungry Americans east of the Mississippi River were eager to settle in the fertile, hospitable lands that Lewis and Clark had discovered in the Oregon country west of Idaho. In the early 1840s, a great migration began as thousands of people walked the Oregon Trail to new homes. The Oregon Trail was a 2,000-mile, six-month journey across prairies and rivers, over mountains, and through deserts.

*During the 1840s, a Belgian missionary named Pierre Jean De Smet helped start several Catholic missions in the Pacific Northwest.*

Between 1840 and 1860, about 253,000 men, women, and children traveled the trail. Some were bound for Oregon, others for California. None of them lingered in Idaho. Instead, they considered their passage through the Snake River Plain to be one of the worst parts of the trip. They usually reached Idaho in late summer, when the blistering heat was at its worst. The pioneers and their pack animals were weary and footsore. Food was often beginning to run short.

*Pioneers heading west on the Oregon Trail crossed the Snake River in southern Idaho.*

Worst of all, water glimmered tantalizingly at the bottom of the Snake River canyon, but in many places the canyon walls were so steep that the thirsty travelers could not get to the water. "If once we are brought safe through this hard place," Sarah Rodgers wrote in her journal while passing through Idaho, "surely we shall never return."

Pioneers on the Oregon Trail were happy to refresh themselves and to renew their supplies at Fort Hall and Fort Boise. They did not look at Idaho as a possible site for settlement—only as an obstacle to the lands farther west. Those who finally established the first settlement in Idaho came from the south.

A religious group called the Church of Jesus Christ of Latter-day Saints—also known as the Mormons—had fled from the East to the desolate wilds of Utah to escape persecution for their unusual beliefs. The Mormons claimed that the founder of their sect was a holy prophet. They also allowed men to have more than one wife. Most Americans found this practice shocking.

The Mormons built a flourishing colony in northern Utah and soon attempted to establish a satellite colony to the north. In 1855, they founded a short-lived settlement called Lemhi in Idaho. It failed, but the Mormons tried again in 1860. Twenty-three families established the town of Franklin, Idaho's first permanent settlement. Soon other Mormon communities had taken root in southern Idaho.

Idaho was not yet called Idaho, however. It was part of the Oregon Territory until 1853, when Congress split the region and created Washington Territory north of the Columbia River. Now the future Idaho was divided between Oregon and Washington territories. When Oregon became a state in 1859, all of Idaho became part of Washington Territory.

## TOWARD STATEHOOD

In 1860, the year Mormons founded Franklin, prospectors discovered gold in the Clearwater River region of central Idaho. The gold rush brought thousands of eager miners from Oregon, California, and the East. After them came merchants, traders, thieves, saloon operators, gamblers, and dance-hall women, all just as eager to take the gold away from the miners. Soon boomtowns such as Orofino, Lewiston, and Florence sprang up in the wild land. Gold strikes to the south, along the Boise River, gave birth to Idaho City and other mining towns. Already Idaho was becoming a place of contrasts and divisions. The rough-and-tumble, lawless mining camps could not have been more different from the orderly, law-abiding Mormon towns.

The government of Washington Territory was located in Olympia, far away from Idaho, and the politicians there found Idaho troublesome and hard to govern. They asked the U.S. Congress to take it off their hands. In 1863, Congress created the Idaho Territory, which included Idaho and parts of Montana and Wyoming. Soon Congress trimmed eastern portions of Idaho away and gave them to other new territories. By 1868, Idaho had acquired its present borders.

Congress chose the name *Idaho Territory* because one of the steamboats that carried miners up the Columbia River to Lewiston was called the *Idaho*. A few years earlier a miner had suggested Idaho as a possible name for Colorado. He claimed that *Idaho* meant "gem of the mountains" in a Native-American language, but in fact it means nothing at all—he had simply made it up. Congress did not know that in 1863, however, and the popular name became attached to the new territory.

*The lure of gold drew prospectors to Idaho.*

# WAY OUT IN IDAHO

The Oregon Short Line was completed in 1884. It ran from Pocatello through the Snake River Valley. The building of this and other railroads opened up the Idaho Territory and helped the lead and silver mining industries.

Come all you jol - ly rail - road men, and I'll sing you if I
can, Of the trials and trib - u - la - tions of a god - less rail - road
man, Who start - ed out from Den - ver,— his for - tune to make
grow, And struck the Or - e - gon Short Line way out in I - da -
ho. Way out in I - da - ho,— way
work - in' on the nar - row gauge way
out in I - da - ho, I'm ho.
out in I - da

I was roaming around in Denver one luckless rainy day,
When Kilpatrick's man, Catcher, stepped up to me and did say,
"I'll lay you down five dollars as quickly as I can,
And you'll hurry up and catch the train, she's starting for Cheyenne."

He laid me down five dollars, like many another man,
And I started for the depot as happy as a clam;
When I got to Pocatello, my troubles began to grow,
A-wading through the sagebrush in frost and rain and snow. *Chorus*

When I got to American Falls, it was there I met Fat Jack.
He said he kept a hotel in a dirty canvas shack.
"We hear you are a stranger and perhaps your funds are low.
Well, yonder stands my hotel tent, the best in Idaho." *Chorus*

I followed my conductor into his hotel tent,
And for one square and hearty meal I paid him my last cent;
But Jack's a jolly fellow, and you'll always find him so,
A-workin' on the narrow-gauge way out in Idaho. *Chorus*

They put me to work next morning with a cranky cuss called Bill,
And they gave me a ten-pound hammer to strike upon a drill.
They said if I didn't like it I could take my shirt and go,
And they'd keep my blanket for my board way out in Idaho. *Chorus*

It filled my heart with pity as I walked along the track
To see so many old bummers with their turkeys on their backs.
They said the work was heavy and the grub they couldn't go.
Around Kilpatrick's tables way out in Idaho. *Chorus*

But now I'm well and happy, down in the harvest camps,
And there I will continue till I make a few more stamps.
I'll go down to New Mexico and I'll marry the girl I know,
And I'll buy me a horse and buggy and go back to Idaho. *Chorus*

"Idaho's early territorial years can only be described as a time of trouble," writes historian Carlos A. Schwantes. In 1864, when the territory's administrators decided to move the capital from Lewiston to Boise, the people of Lewiston rebelled and placed the territorial seal under armed guard. Citizens from Boise tried to steal it. Eventually the capital did move, but the unforgiving people of Lewiston repeatedly tried to rejoin their part of Idaho with Washington.

The poor performance of Idaho's territorial governors also caused problems. The territory had sixteen governors in twenty-seven years. Four failed to take office. Six governors spent less than a year—some only a few days—in Idaho. Government officials also stole large sums of money from the territorial treasury.

These administrative troubles were nothing compared to the turmoil faced by Idaho's Native Americans, however. They suffered terribly from new diseases introduced by the whites. The inrush of miners, settlers, and livestock occupied more and more of the land that the Native Americans needed to support their traditional way of life. U.S. Army and government officials began forcing the Native Americans onto reservations.

Then, in 1863, tragedy struck southwestern Idaho. Starving Shoshone-Bannock Indians had been raiding wagon trains and the town of Franklin. A group of California volunteers marched into the region and attacked a Shoshone band at Bear River. Twenty-two Californians died. The death toll among the Native Americans was far higher. Utah settlers visited the battlefield and counted 368 dead Native Americans, including nearly 90 women and children. After this disaster, the Shoshone-Bannock agreed to move onto the Fort Hall Reservation.

The Nez Perce met a similar fate in 1877. Some Nez Perce had moved onto the Lapwai Reservation near the Clearwater River, but others claimed the right to live in their traditional homeland, the Wallowa Valley of northeastern Oregon. Settlers wanted the valley, however, so the federal government told the army to move the Nez Perce to Idaho. A fight broke out, and eight hundred Native Americans, led by Chief Joseph, fled through the mountains toward Canada. The pursuing soldiers caught up with them in Montana. Chief Joseph is supposed to have declared, "My heart is sick and sad. From where the sun now stands I will fight no more forever." Some of the Nez Perce who followed Joseph eventually ended up in Idaho, although Chief Joseph lived out his days on a reservation in Washington.

*This photograph of Chief Joseph of the Nez Perce was taken in 1903.*

Idaho's last Native-American uprisings occurred in the late 1870s, as Native Americans in southern Idaho struggled in vain to hold back the rising tide of settlers. Soon all of Idaho's Native Americans were confined to reservations. In the coming years, the government repeatedly reduced the size of these reservations to please incoming white settlers, ranchers, and miners who demanded more and more of Idaho for their own.

By the late 1880s, the Idaho Territory had about 90,000 residents. They were clamoring for statehood—although they did not all want to be in the *same* state. Some residents in the north wanted to join Washington State, created in 1889. Congress came close to dividing the Idaho Territory between Washington and Nevada, but the people of southern Idaho were horrified by the idea of becoming part of Nevada, which had a reputation for crooked politics. The territory's governor convinced President Grover Cleveland that Idaho should remain united. In 1890, Congress made Idaho the nation's forty-third state.

## THE TWENTIETH CENTURY AND BEYOND

During its first years of statehood, Idaho was plagued by labor struggles as miners fought to improve their wages and working conditions.

**POPULATION GROWTH: 1870–2000**

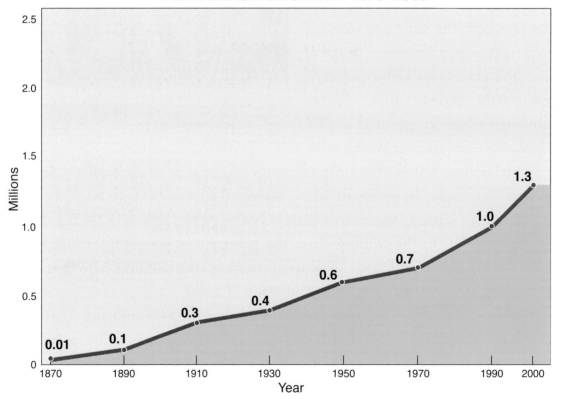

The miners formed organizations called unions, which sometimes went on strike. Union members refused to work until their demands were met. Clashes between striking mine workers and stubborn mine owners frequently flared into violence. In 1892, striking miners in the Coeur d'Alene region dynamited a mill, and six people died. Then, in 1899, the union attacked a mining company that had refused to hire union workers and blew the company's offices to bits. Federal troops arrested hundreds of miners. A few years later, an assassin killed Governor Frank Steunenberg and claimed that union officials had hired him. The officials were found not guilty in a sensational 1907 trial, and the era of Idaho's worst mining wars drew to an end.

By this time, new industries were developing. In the early 1900s, timber companies started buying and logging large tracts of Idaho land. Despite raging forest fires in 1910 that consumed 3 million acres of trees, the timber industry steadily grew in importance. Agriculture also grew. As early as the days of Henry Spalding's Lapwai mission, farmers had found that potatoes grew well in Idaho's sandy soil. By 1929, the state was producing 25 million bushels of spuds a year.

*Loggers working in Cataldo Mission prepare to haul their harvest to the sawmill.*

The worldwide economic depression of the 1930s caused great misery in Idaho. As the price of minerals, timber, and farm produce dropped, Idahoans' incomes also plummeted. Some people grew so desperate that they began setting fires so that they could earn a few dollars by serving on the emergency crews that put the fires out.

*These children lived on a farm in Oneida County in 1936, when Idaho and the entire country were in the grip of the Great Depression.*

In the midst of the depression, however, one sign of a bright new future appeared on the horizon. A railroad executive who wanted to develop a European-style ski resort in the United States chose a site near the old Idaho mining town of Ketchum. The railroad poured development money into the area, and the luxury resort of Sun Valley was born in 1938. It was a hint of the coming boom in outdoor sports and the rise of tourism.

*Sun Valley attracted skiers from across the nation. This photograph was taken in 1939.*

An entirely different kind of camp rose in 1942 at Minidoka, north of Twin Falls. It was one of many relocation centers for Japanese Americans from the West Coast during World War II. Driven by the suspicion that people of Japanese descent would support Japan, American's enemy in the war, the federal government overrode their civil rights and placed them in camps such as Minidoka. Nearly ten thousand Japanese Americans were confined at Minidoka, where they lived in barracks covered in tar paper and surrounded by barbed wire. The 1,200 Japanese Americans living in Idaho at the outbreak of the war were not put into the camps, but they did suffer from anti-Japanese prejudice. After the war ended in 1945, some of the relocated people from the West Coast stayed in Idaho and enlarged the state's Japanese-American community.

*At the Minidoka Relocation Center, the children of Japanese Americans who were imprisoned during World War II attended a government-run school.*

Idaho contributed a milestone to history in 1951, when a power plant at a research center now called the Idaho National Laboratory (INL) became the first place in the world to produce electricity from atomic energy. The nearby town of Arco still proudly boasts that it was the first town lit by nuclear power. Again, however, progress came at a price. By the late 1980s, nuclear waste had made INL one of the nation's most dangerously contaminated sites.

*The turbine and generator of the nuclear power plant at Arco produced the first useful energy from nuclear power. The plant supplied the town's electricity.*

In the 1970s, a century after the last of Idaho's Native-American uprisings, a war broke out in the state. In a symbolic gesture, the Kutenai tribe—Idaho's smallest and northernmost Native-American group, living just south of the Canadian border—declared war on the United States. The Kutenai were angry because, unlike Idaho's other tribes, they had never received reservation land from the federal government. They set up roadblocks on the roads leading into their area and charged a toll of ten cents to let cars through. The "Kutenai war" made national news and led President Gerald Ford to grant the Kutenai a small reservation, which has been expanded.

During the final decades of the twentieth century, Idaho made national news because of actions by the state's white supremacists. These are people who believe in the superiority of the white race and sometimes commit hate crimes or other illegal actions driven by that belief. Although white supremacists and their supporters made up only a small number of Idahoans, they drew negative publicity to the state.

Much of the negative publicity centered on Aryan Nations, a white supremacy church, political organization, and community founded in 1974 near Hayden, Idaho, by Richard Butler. Some of Butler's followers were convicted of crimes such as murder, bombing, and armed robbery. The group's influence crumbled after its security guards assaulted a woman and her son, who later won a large court settlement from Aryan Nations. When Butler died in 2004, his group was on the decline, although it still held occasional gatherings in northern Idaho. Aryan Nations parades often brought out large numbers of protestors who opposed the racism and violence of the white supremacists. Tony Stewart, who helped organize the Kootenai County Task Force on Human Relations to counteract the Aryan Nations movement in the early 1980s, has said that it will take time to erase the stain on Idaho's reputation.

One of the biggest—and most tragic—events in Idaho in the 1990s was indirectly linked to the Aryan Nations. Randy Weaver, who lived in a cabin in northern Idaho with his family, had attended a few Aryan Nations functions but was not a member of the group. In 1990 an agent of the U.S. Bureau of Alcohol, Tobacco and Firearms tried to persuade Weaver to spy on Aryan Nations for the government. Weaver refused and later was arrested on charges of selling illegal guns. In 1992, after Weaver refused to appear in court to answer the charges, federal marshals laid seige to his cabin in Ruby Ridge. In a gunfight, Weaver's son and wife, as well as a federal marshal were killed. The

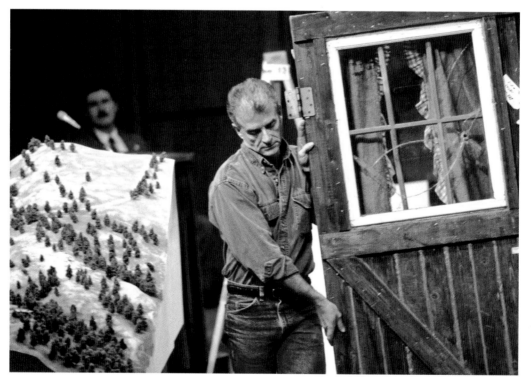

*At a U.S. Senate hearing in Washington, D.C., Randy Weaver holds the door from his Ruby Ridge home. Weaver's wife died when an FBI sniper fired through the door.*

Ruby Ridge disaster became a rallying point for people who oppose the federal government. After an investigation, the U.S. Senate concluded that federal agents had made a series of flawed decisions. The Weavers later were granted settlements in a case against the federal government.

By the early years of the twenty-first century, the political and social storms of the 1990s had quieted considerably. One long-standing dispute reached a new settlement in 2005, when the state made a water agreement with the Nez Perce Indians. For years, the Nez Perce had claimed that old treaties gave them control of nearly all the water in the Snake River basin, a dry area of southern Idaho where water is scarce. The 2005 legislation created a thirty-year agreement in which the Nez Perce gave up their claim to much of the Snake River water in exchange for $80 million and a guaranteed amount of water from the Clearwater River each year. Now the state will determine how the precious resource of Snake River water will be used for agriculture and other developments over the next three decades.

Life in Idaho reflects the trends that have met and mingled in the state since the middle of the twentieth century. A rush of dam building led to plentiful electricity and more irrigation—but also drew criticism from the growing environmental movement after the 1970s. The state's wilderness has attracted ever-growing numbers of admiring visitors and tourist dollars—but timber and mining companies also want to claim their piece of the land. People from outside are moving into Idaho. Some work in new, high-technology firms in Boise or other fast-growing cities. Others hope to return to the pioneer lifestyle in small rural towns or on isolated homesteads. As Idaho moves into its second century of statehood, it remains a place of differing points of view, a jumble of contradictions.

## Chapter Three

# North, South—and West

People in the Gem State often talk of two Idahos. Many times they mean north Idaho and south Idaho. Sometimes they mean city and country—Boise and its suburbs contrasted with the rural parts of the state. Yet other times they mean new Idaho and old Idaho—newcomers from recent years and people whose roots in the state go back a generation or more.

Despite these contrasts, one thing is true everywhere in Idaho: It is part of the West. Scuffed boots and weathered pickup trucks are part of the scenery. Horseback riding and hunting are familiar parts of life for lots of people, including teenagers.

You'll be reminded that you're in the West as you drive up a rutted mountain road in Clearwater National Forest. Most of the traffic signs are bullet-riddled, because a lot of gun-totin' Westerners seem to regard signs as targets. Or you may be driving along Interstate 84 on a windy February day, heading for the urban attractions of Boise, when suddenly a herd of golden-brown tumbleweeds appears on the horizon. Traffic stops while they whirl and bound across four lanes. At times like these, even someone in a business suit feels like a cowboy.

*For this cowgirl and many other Idahoans, riding is a way of life. Although more people live in cities than in the country, the Western spirit is alive and well in Idaho.*

## A STATE WITH THREE CAPITALS

Idahoans joke that theirs is the only state with three capitals—Boise, Spokane, and Salt Lake City. There is some truth to the joke. Idaho's panhandle is geographically similar to that of eastern Washington, and many people there remember that their ancestors wanted to be part of Washington, not Idaho. When people in Coeur d'Alene or Kellogg have an errand to do in a bigger city, it's much easier for them to drive to Spokane, just across the border in Washington, than to spend hours traveling to Boise. Geography is still a powerful barrier to traveling in Idaho. Several east-west routes cross the state, but only one paved road, Highway 95, runs north to south the entire way. The highway is squeezed between the bulk of the central mountains and the gorge of Hells Canyon.

In the same way, many people in rural southeastern Idaho feel culturally and geographically closer to Utah, and to its nearby capital in Salt Lake City, than to Boise. Mormons from Utah settled much of southeastern Idaho. Mormon heritage is still strong in the region.

Religion and church are important parts of daily life for many Idahoans. Today Idaho has more Mormons than any state except Utah, and more of Idaho's churchgoers belong to the Church of Jesus Christ of Latter-day Saints than to any other church. In 2004, nearly 23 percent of Idahoans identified themselves as Mormons. The Roman Catholic faith also has many followers, especially in the north. In 2004, more than 14 percent of the state's inhabitants were Catholic. This is a legacy of the early Catholic missions. It is also the result of a recent increase in immigrants from Mexico and other largely Catholic nations of Latin America. Protestant churches, including some fundamentalist groups, are also active in Idaho.

## ETHNIC IDAHO

As of 2006, according to the U.S. Census Bureau, Idaho's population is at just under 1.47 million. This is not a very large piece of the total U.S. population, which was just under 300 million in the same year. Idaho's population may be small, but it is growing. Between 2000 and 2006, the state's population increased by 13.3 percent, compared with a nationwide increase of 6.4 percent. Between 2005 and 2006, Idaho's population grew by 2.6 percent. This makes Idaho the third-fastest-growing state in the country after Arizona and Nevada. About a third of the population increase came from people born in Idaho. The other two-thirds happened because people moved to Idaho from other places.

Word of Idaho's attractions seems to be getting out. As early as 1998, a motel keeper in Twin Falls saw signs of growth but was not concerned about it. "It's only been in the last couple of years that we've had more than a million people here," he remarked. He compared life in Idaho to memories of a trip he had taken to Chicago thirty years earlier. "So many people—who could live like that?" he asked, shaking his head.

Some people move to Idaho because it has exactly what they want in terms of landscape and a way of life. Other newcomers find that Idaho forces them to make some adjustments. After one young Asian-American woman moved from San Francisco to Boise to take a job she loves, she discovered that it was more challenging than she had expected to live in a state with very few Asian Americans. She became more aware of being a minority than she had ever been.

According to the U.S. Census Bureau's 2005 American Community Survey, Idaho is 92 percent white. Less than 3 percent of Idahoans are African American, Asian American, Pacific Islander, or Native American put together. Outside Boise and the other urban centers of the Snake River Plain, it is rare to see a person of color.

# ETHNIC IDAHO

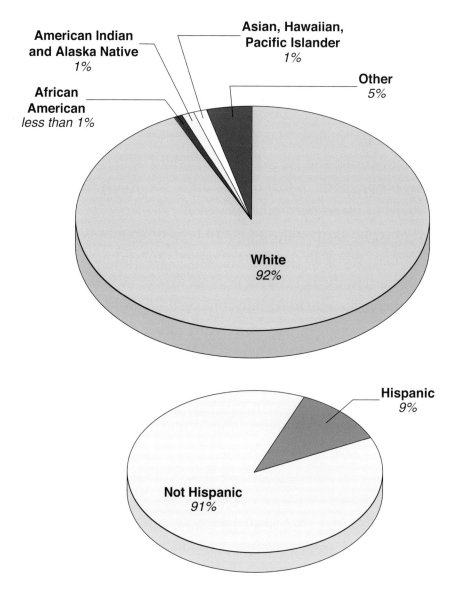

**American Indian and Alaska Native**
*1%*

**Asian, Hawaiian, Pacific Islander**
*1%*

**African American**
*less than 1%*

**Other**
*5%*

**White**
*92%*

**Hispanic**
*9%*

**Not Hispanic**
*91%*

*Note: A person of Cuban, Mexican, Puerto Rican, South or Central American, or other Spanish culture or origin, regardless of race, is defined as Hispanic.*

Less than 1 percent of Idaho's population is Native American. The federal government recognizes five tribal identities: Kutenai (also spelled Kootenai), Coeur d'Alene, Nez Perce, Shoshone-Bannock, and Shoshone-Paiute. Many, but not all, of Idaho's Native Americans live on the state's five reservations. They hold various events—such as Chief Lookingglass Days in Kamiah, a town on the Nez Perce Reservation, and the Shoshone-Bannock Indian Festival in Fort Hall—to celebrate their heritage and to attract tourists. In recent years, operating gambling casinos has become a major economic activity for Native Americans in Idaho, as in many other states.

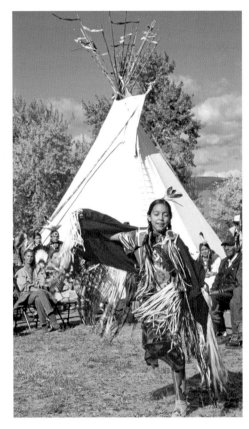

*A Lemhi-Shoshone girl performs a traditional butterfly dance at a ceremony in Salmon.*

Idaho's largest minority is its Hispanic, or Latino, population. Hispanics made up about 9.5 percent of the total state population in 2006. Nearly a fourth of all new residents in Idaho are Hispanic. Idaho has the fifteenth-largest percentage of Latinos of any state in the country. "Hispanics are an important segment of Idaho's economy, supplying critical manpower to keep the state's expansion going and providing businesses with a significant market for goods and services," Roger Madsen, the state's director of commerce and labor, said in 2007.

Some of the Hispanic newcomers are migrant workers who came to pick crops and decided to stay. Polo Yanez of Rexburg operates a radio station to serve the needs of Spanish-speaking residents. Broadcasted in Spanish, the station is supported by advertisements from local Hispanic-owned businesses. Yanez remembers how hard it was for him to feel good about his Hispanic identity after moving from Texas to Blackfoot, Idaho, in 1971. "I had a pretty bad time," he recalls. "I never got adjusted." Today Yanez operates his radio station partly as a business and partly as a service to his fellow Hispanic Idahoans. "It promotes self-confidence in the community," he says.

*A farm worker of Latino descent delivers gourds to a market.*

Idaho is home to several thousand people of Basque heritage. Their ancestors moved to Idaho from the mountains of northern Spain between 1890 and 1920 to work as sheepherders, miners, and construction laborers. Many of the immigrants sent for their wives and families to join them. Soon they had created a community that kept the Basque language and customs alive in the Boise area. Today the Basque Museum and Cultural Center in Boise honors those early settlers and serves as a focus for Idahoans of Basque descent.

Despite the growing Hispanic presence in Idaho and the long Native-American history in the state, many Idahoans live in small communities with very little ethnic diversity. This way of life can be comforting, but it also has a dark side. People who are not exposed to change and diversity can become intolerant and prejudiced. This is one

*Dancers at a festival in Boise celebrate the heritage of the Basque, people descended from immigrants who moved to Idaho from the Pyrenees Mountains of northern Spain.*

reason that groups promoting white supremacy established themselves in northern Idaho. As one Lewiston woman points out, however, "They're here, but they're not in the majority. Most of us are deeply embarrassed to have our state identified with hatred and violence."

## RECREATION AND CULTURE

"Throughout Idaho are men who have settled in the state and natives who refuse to leave simply because the side rewards of living there are greater than the greater money they might make outside. They like small towns and small-city associations, and they like free space, and they fill their eyes with grandeur and their ears with the great silence of the mountains." A. B. Guthrie wrote these words for *Holiday* magazine in 1954. To many Idahoans they still ring true.

The people of Idaho like living in a place where neighbors know each other and no one passes by a stranded motorist on a winter road. They like being close to wild land and the freedom it represents. Even a Boise office worker is just a short drive from pristine forests and quiet mountain paths. One accountant there keeps his snowboard in his office for after-work jaunts to the nearby hills. "Maybe I'll only take it out three or four times a year," he admits. "But it's just cool to know I *can*."

Many of Idaho's fairs, festivals, and events honor the state's pioneer heritage. Coeur d'Alene Indians celebrate a pilgrimage in which they reenact the arrival of the Black Robes, the early Catholic missionaries. Lewiston hosts one of Idaho's many rodeos. Orofino has Lumberjack Days, in which loggers from many states compete in such events as logrolling. At the Mountain Man Rendezvous, held at Massacre Rocks State Park near American Falls, people relive the days of the fur trappers with knife-throwing contests and tepee villages. Every June, fiddlers

*A rodeo in Hailey is one of many annual events in which Idahoans and visitors relive the state's pioneer and frontier days.*

from around the world gather in the farming town of Weiser for the National Oldtime Fiddlers' Contest, where music fills the air and toes tap late into the night.

Other events celebrate the land and its bounty. Idaho hosts the Cherry Festival at harvesttime in Emmett, the Apple Blossom Festival in Payette, and, of course, Idaho Annual Spud Day, celebrated in the potato-growing community of Shelley. Seasonal events range from summer white-water kayak "rodeos" on the Payette River to Christmastime tree lightings and reenactments of pioneer holidays.

Idaho's cultural life is as rich and varied as its landscape. Boise has professional ballet, symphony, and opera companies as well as museums, theaters, and a lively art gallery scene. Cultural life is not confined to the capital, however. In many communities, events such as the Lionel Hampton Jazz Festival, the Sun Valley Summer Symphony, and the Idaho Shakespeare Festival entertain and enlighten Idahoans.

*A junior fiddler wields his bow in the Old Time Fiddlers' Contest in Weiser, one of the nation's top fiddling events.*

The cultural life of Idaho is linked to the state's network of colleges and universities, many of which host drama programs, music groups, film clubs, and other cultural activities. State universities include the University of Idaho in Moscow, Idaho State University in Pocatello, and Boise State University. The state colleges are the College of Southern Idaho in Twin Falls, Eastern Idaho Technical College in Idaho Falls, Lewis-Clark State College in Lewiston, North Idaho College in Coeur d'Alene, and the College of Western Idaho in Nampa (approved by voters in 2007). There are also a number of private colleges and universities throughout the state.

*Ballet is one of many artistic and cultural offerings in Boise, the state's capital and largest city.*

## AN AMERICAN PARADISE?

With its homespun communities, its natural beauty, and a generous helping of culture, is Idaho an American paradise? Ask the people who are flocking to buy homes in the Teton Valley in the eastern part of the state. During the 1990s, Teton County's population grew faster than that of any other Idaho county. It rose by 54 percent in just seven years. Growth has not been painless, however. One farmer made headlines when, after losing a battle to block a housing development on what used to be farmland, he put up a sign warning potential buyers of the hazards of rural life, such as cow manure and barnyard smells.

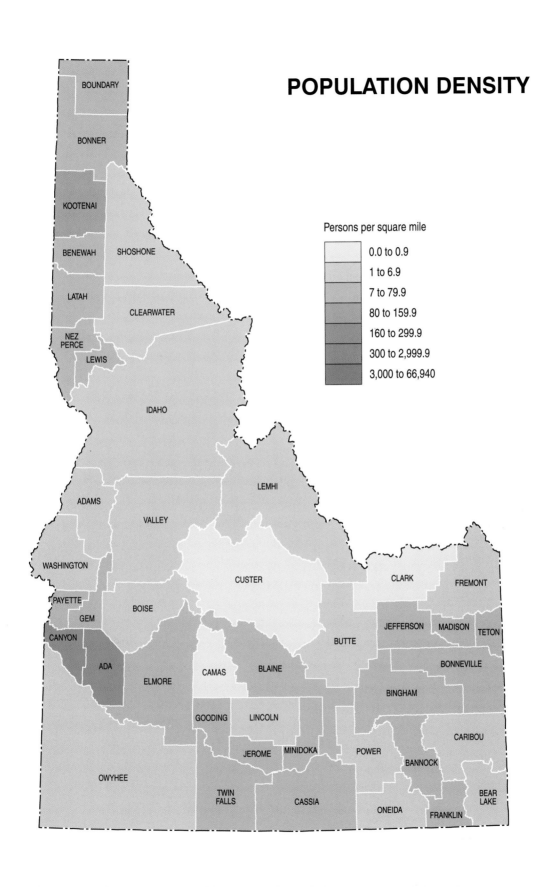

# POPULATION DENSITY

BOUNDARY

BONNER

KOOTENAI

BENEWAH

SHOSHONE

LATAH

CLEARWATER

NEZ PERCE

LEWIS

IDAHO

LEMHI

ADAMS

VALLEY

WASHINGTON

CUSTER

CLARK

FREMONT

PAYETTE

BOISE

GEM

JEFFERSON

MADISON

TETON

CANYON

BUTTE

BONNEVILLE

ADA

CAMAS

BLAINE

ELMORE

BINGHAM

GOODING

LINCOLN

CARIBOU

JEROME

MINIDOKA

POWER

BANNOCK

OWYHEE

TWIN FALLS

CASSIA

ONEIDA

FRANKLIN

BEAR LAKE

Persons per square mile

0.0 to 0.9

1 to 6.9

7 to 79.9

80 to 159.9

160 to 299.9

300 to 2,999.9

3,000 to 66,940

## WINTER CARNIVAL

On the shore of beautiful Payette Lake in west-central Idaho is the town of McCall. In summer it is a paradise of swimming, boating, fishing, and sunny outdoor fun. But what about winter? In 1924, a resident of McCall came up with a plan to banish the midwinter doldrums: dogsled races. It was the beginning of a yearly tradition. Local people began building snow sculptures, and in the 1960s a sculpture contest became an official part of the festivities.

Today the McCall Winter Carnival is one of Idaho's liveliest events. The carnival includes many different snow-sculpting competitions, ranging from children's contests to a competition that draws professional snow sculptors from around the world. A visitor to McCall during the festival should not be surprised to see a giant snow cowboy riding an even bigger sea serpent or a lumbering family of two-story-tall polar bears. The 2007 carnival, whose theme was Wonders of the World, featured massive snow sculptures of the Taj Mahal, Mount Rushmore, the Sphinx in Egypt, and Australia's Great Barrier Reef.

The conflict between farmers and property developers illustrates the tension between the forces that are changing Idaho and the people who want to keep it unchanged. Idaho already had changed a great deal since 1900, however, when 6 percent of its people lived in cities and 94 percent lived in the country. A U.S. Census Bureau estimate in 2006 showed that almost 85 percent of Idaho's population lived in its eleven largest urban areas. Like the United States as a whole, Idaho had become largely urban, not rural.

The fastest-growing urban area is the Boise metropolitan district, which includes four counties and the nearby city of Nampa, one of the fastest-growing communities in the state. According to a 2007 report from the U.S. Census Bureau, Boise-Nampa ranked sixteenth among the nation's one hundred fastest-growing metropolitan areas, while Coeur d'Alene ranked twentieth and Idaho Falls was forty-fourth.

Idaho's cities may be growing, but some of its small towns are dying. The state's landscape is dotted with shrinking communities like King Hill on the Snake River Plain. "It was a good place to raise your children," recalls Peggy Marnock, who emigrated from Scotland in the early 1930s. "I'll bet there's not a hundred people here now. Mostly retired folks."

To some people, paradise means doing it your own way, and Idaho has plenty of room for them. In 1993, Alanna Lefsaker wrote about her family's experiences in Idaho: "Seven years [we] were in a very remote area near Hells Canyon and we loved it, but our kids turned into teens and [being] 60 miles from the nearest town made it a little difficult for them to make friends, so we now live 12 miles from town on 155 acres. We like it here, too. It's almost as remote since we're at the end of the road and the road is a very rough one." For many Idahoans, the rough road is the road to contentment.

## Chapter Four

# Making Decisions

Before it could become a state, Idaho needed a constitution to serve as its basis of law and government. In 1889, the people of the territory created such a constitution. Although it has changed over the years, Idaho's original constitution remains the framework of government within the state. It represents Idahoans' best effort to set forth rules and values that all people support.

Like the federal government and the governments of other states, Idaho's government consists of three branches: executive, legislative, and judicial. Each branch has its own responsibilities. Effective government requires that the three branches work together in balance.

## THE EXECUTIVE BRANCH

The executive branch acts as the overseer, or administrator, of government. Idaho's chief executive is its governor, who has three principal responsibilities. One is overseeing the smooth operation of all of the departments and agencies that administer laws and do the state's work. Another is working with state legislators in the lawmaking process. Finally, the governor

*Idaho's state government is based in the capitol building in Boise. Completed in 1913, the building has a dome that reaches a height of 208 feet.*

represents Idaho at the national level by communicating the state's needs to the president. Idaho voters elect the governor to a term of four years.

Idaho has had some noteworthy governors. Moses Alexander, who served from 1915 to 1919, was the first Jewish governor in the United States. Cecil Andrus served four terms as governor in the 1970s, 1980s, and 1990s. As governor he fought to control the mining industry and to establish the Sawtooth and Hells Canyon national recreation areas. Andrus also served in the federal government. As U.S. secretary of the interior from 1977 to 1981, he helped protect wilderness land in Alaska.

*Cecil Andrus, a key figure in state and national political life for decades, is shown here during his 1986 campaign for governor.*

In 2006, Idahoans elected Republican C. L. "Butch" Otter as their governor in a close contest. Otter said, "My goal as your Governor is to empower Idaho to be all that America was meant to be, and to empower Idahoans to be the architects of their own destiny." Governor Otter is known as a strong supporter of farming and hunting organizations. For example, he has opposed the reintroduction of gray wolves to Idaho because of the belief that they harm the hunting industry by killing elk and other game animals. Otter also has promoted the development of alternative energy in Idaho. He has signed several new tax laws designed to help citizens start wind farms to harness the power of wind and turn it into electricity.

*C. L. "Butch" Otter, a Republican, became governor of Idaho in 2006.*

Other important elected officials of the executive branch are the lieutenant governor, the secretary of state, the state controller, the state treasurer, the attorney general, and the superintendent of public instruction. These officials are responsible for overseeing the departments of government that carry out Idaho's laws. Because Idaho contains one of the nation's greatest percentages of federally owned land, the state's officials must work frequently and closely with federal officials and agencies. The controller pays the state's bills, and the treasurer manages and invests the state's money.

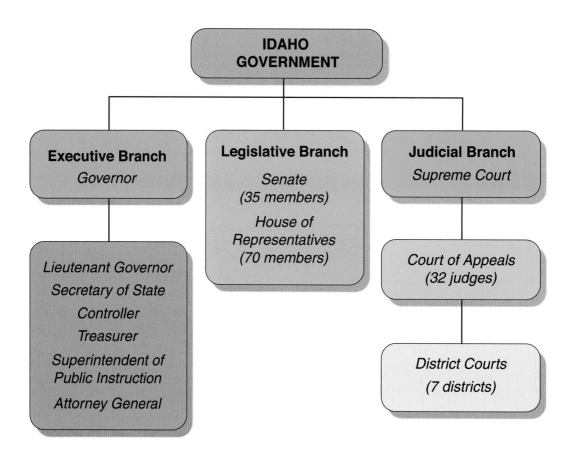

## THE LEGISLATURE

The legislative branch, or legislature, makes laws for the state. Idaho's legislature consists of two bodies, the senate and the house of representatives. The state is divided into thirty-five legislative districts. Voters in each district elect one senator and two representatives for two-year terms. Members of the legislature form committees to develop laws dealing with education, finance, the environment, health and welfare, transportation, defense, local government, and agricultural affairs.

The legislature introduces and votes on bills, which are proposals involving laws or the spending of public funds. Both the senate and the house of representatives must approve a bill in order to pass it. The bill becomes law when the governor signs it. Even if the governor doesn't sign it, a bill can become law if two-thirds of the lawmakers in each body of the legislature approve it.

## THE JUDICIAL SYSTEM

The judicial branch of government is responsible for interpreting the law. The first level of the judicial system consists of general district courts. The district court judges, elected to four-year terms, hear civil and criminal cases. Their decisions may be appealed in the court of appeals, which consists of three elected judges who serve six-year terms. The state's highest court is the Idaho Supreme Court, which hears cases referred from the court of appeals and decides cases related to the state constitution. The five supreme court justices are elected to six-year terms.

## FIGHTING FOR CONTROL

Some of Idaho's hottest political issues in recent years have roots that reach far into the past. Old treaties between the U.S. government and the

Indians of Idaho, as well as federal laws that define Native Americans' rights, have become the subject of new disputes. At the heart of these debates is the question of who really owns Idaho's land.

An 1855 treaty established the Nez Perce Reservation east of Lewiston. In 1893, the reservation was opened to white homesteading and now contains several towns. Since the 1990s, the reservation has experienced an economic revival, thanks in large part to the opening of several casinos. Starting in the late 1990s, however, there has been periodic disagreement between the members of the Nez Perce tribe and the non-Indian Idahoans who live and work within the reservation. Nearly 90 percent of the reservation now belongs to non-Indians or to government agencies.

The Nez Perce tribe claims the right to control reservation land. Its leaders requested that a greater percentage of Indians be employed on public projects on the reservation. Non-Indian residents and town officials countered that the old reservation boundaries no longer apply. They rejected Nez Perce tribal codes and laws about land use and ownership. Jaime Pinkham, an elected official of the tribe, called this response "the most serous threat [the Nez Perce] community has faced in my lifetime." The tribe warned that if its claim to control of the reservation is not honored, it could cancel the rights-of-way for roads on the reservation. The Nez Perce also threatened to interfere with the gas, electric, telephone, and water lines that cross the reservation and provide necessary services to north-central Idaho.

Several dozen non-Indian groups—including city and county governments, school districts, and citizen groups—formed the North Central Idaho Jurisdictional Alliance to oppose the Native Americans' claims of control. "As far as I'm concerned," said one frustrated non-Indian resident, "the reservation should be no more." On the other hand, tribal spokesperson Sam Penney said, "We are a responsible government."

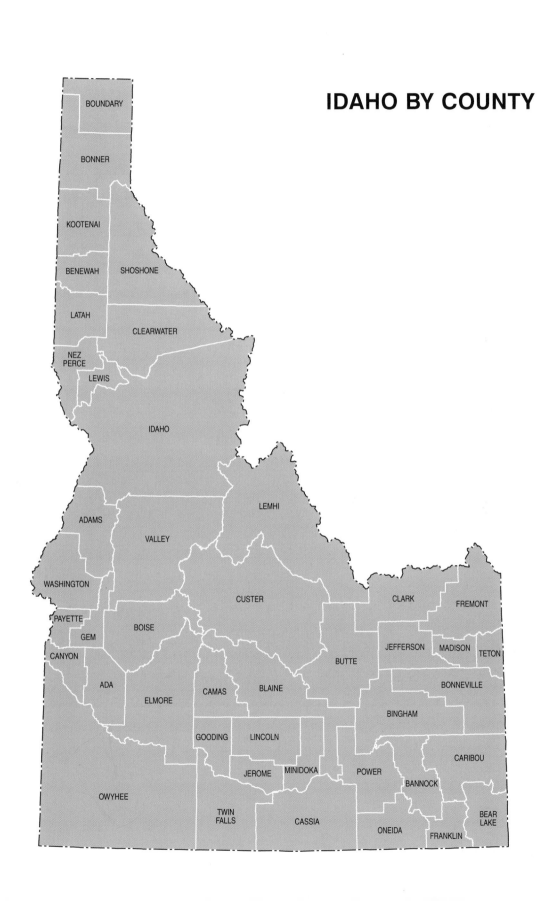

**IDAHO BY COUNTY**

BOUNDARY

BONNER

KOOTENAI

BENEWAH

SHOSHONE

LATAH

CLEARWATER

NEZ PERCE

LEWIS

IDAHO

LEMHI

ADAMS

VALLEY

WASHINGTON

CUSTER

CLARK

FREMONT

PAYETTE

BOISE

JEFFERSON

MADISON

TETON

GEM

CANYON

BUTTE

BONNEVILLE

ADA

CAMAS

BLAINE

ELMORE

BINGHAM

GOODING

LINCOLN

CARIBOU

JEROME

MINIDOKA

POWER

BANNOCK

OWYHEE

TWIN FALLS

CASSIA

ONEIDA

FRANKLIN

BEAR LAKE

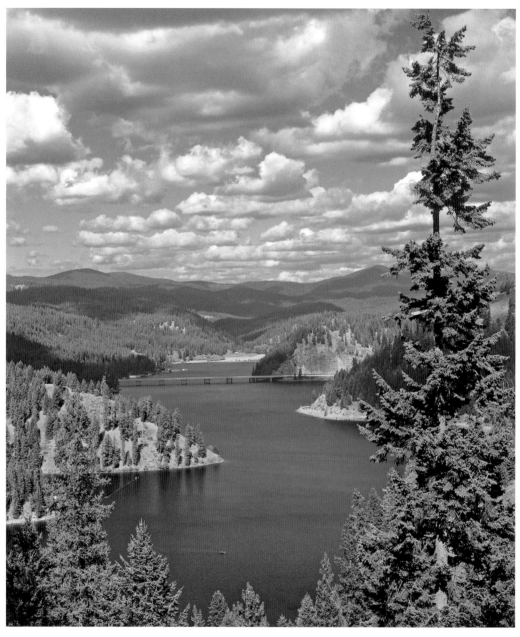

*Lake Coeur d'Alene, one of Idaho's scenic treasures, has also been the subject of a lawsuit over tribal ownership.*

She added that the Nez Perce hope to settle the ownership dispute through conversations with their non-Indian neighbors, not through lawsuits. Both sides realize that resolving the conflict will be a long, difficult process that might reach the U.S. Supreme Court. Meanwhile, tribes elsewhere in Idaho and throughout the West are paying close attention to events at the Nez Perce Reservation. The situation might set an example for similar conflicts on other Native American lands.

Lake Coeur d'Alene was the subject of a tug-of-war that did go to the U.S. Supreme Court in 2001. The court upheld a claim by the Coeur d'Alene tribe that an 1873 executive order by President Ulysses S. Grant gave the tribe ownership of the southern third of the lake. Fees for fishing and launching boats in that part of the lake now go to the tribe, not to the state. The tribe is seeking damages from mining companies and other industries that polluted the lake in the past. "[The lake] must and will be protected for the benefit of our regional economy, to be sure," said tribal spokesman Ernie Stensgar. "But it must also be protected for the unborn generations, Indian and non-Indian, who will live and thrive here."

## Chapter Five

# Growing Industries

Many Idahoans like to think of themselves as living off the land. The truth is, however, that a growing number of residents earn their living in offices and factories. In terms of the amount of money earned, Idaho's top economic activity is manufacturing—everything from construction equipment to high-technology electronic components such as computer chips and laser printers. Engineering and research also are booming in Idaho. While many Idahoans work for private high-tech firms, the government-run Idaho National Laboratory employs several thousand scientists and engineers.

Science and technology make up the biggest piece of Idaho's manufacturing economy. More than 70 percent of the dollar value of the state's exports comes from high-technology products such as semi-conductor chips for electronic equipment. More than a quarter of the state's overall income is from the sale of technology-related goods and services. Manufacture of recreational vehicles and trailers is on the rise in Idaho. The construction, real-estate, and health-care industries also have grown in recent years.

*Although Idaho's economy is shifting toward technology and services, industry remains strong. Pictured here is a nitrogen plant in Nampa.*

## IDAHO WORKFORCE

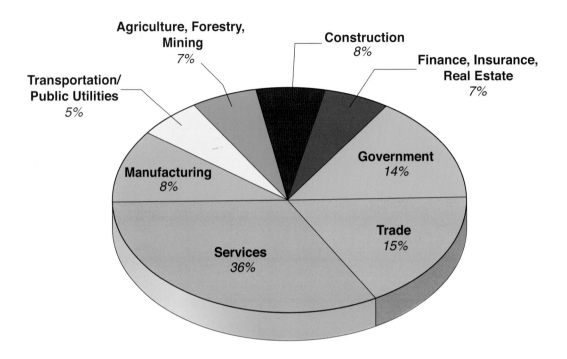

**Agriculture, Forestry, Mining** 7%

**Construction** 8%

**Finance, Insurance, Real Estate** 7%

**Transportation/ Public Utilities** 5%

**Government** 14%

**Manufacturing** 8%

**Trade** 15%

**Services** 36%

## AGRICULTURE: POTATOES AND MORE

In the early twentieth century, agriculture dominated Idaho's economy. Today it accounts for just 5 percent of the state's gross yearly production, but farming is still an important part of Idaho's identity. Closely related to agriculture is one of the state's key industries, food processing—the canning, freezing, and packaging of food.

For many people around the nation and the world, Idaho *is* agriculture. More specifically, it is the potato. Over the years the state has exported millions of bags of spuds, all proudly labeled IDAHO GROWN. Even Idaho's license plate promotes the humble tuber through its slogan "Famous Potatoes."

*Growing conditions in southern Idaho are perfect for potatoes, the state's best-known agricultural product.*

One-third of all the potatoes grown in the United States come from Idaho. In 2006, Idaho potato farmers earned about $712 million for approximately 12 billion pounds of potatoes. Most of the state's potatoes are grown on the Snake River Plain. During harvest time everyone pitches in to bring in the crop. Each fall, ten of the state's school districts give children time off to help with the potato harvest on their family farms. "I like doing it," said an eleven-year-old as he sorts spuds in the cellar of his uncle's barn. "I might want to have my own farm someday, so this is good experience. Besides, it's more fun than being in school. This afternoon I'm going out in the fields on the trucks."

In 2006, the U.S. Department of Agriculture reported some disturbing news. Potatoes from one region of Idaho were found to contain potato cyst nematodes, small worms that eat the roots of potato plants. It was the first time that this pest, found in South America and Europe, was discovered in the United States. Canada, Mexico, and Japan immediately banned the import of fresh potatoes from Idaho for fear that the nematodes would infect their own potato fields.

Although the nematodes do not damage potatoes themselves, they can severely reduce the productivity of potato fields. Agricultural scientists quarantined the Idaho fields in question and set out to destroy the nematodes on about 950 acres. It could take years to be certain that the pest has not spread to other fields. In the meantime, Canada and Mexico lifted their bans. Japan is also considering lifting its ban.

Despite the nematode problem, the future of the potato looks good—the average American eats about 138 pounds of spuds a year, including chips and fries. The famous potato is not Idaho's only crop, however. Farmers in forty-two of the state's forty-four counties grow wheat. The state's annual wheat crop would fill a train stretching 340 miles from Boise to Salt Lake City. Peas, lentils, sugar beets, and plums are other leading crops. Idaho also ranks third in the nation as a producer of onions, barley, mint, and hops (a plant used in beer making).

## OVEN-ROASTED JO-JOS

Jo-jos are roasted potato chunks—something like French fries but bigger, better, and a lot less greasy. The best way to make them is with a couple of large, firm Idaho spuds. Have an adult help you make your jo-jos.

Preheat your oven to 400 degrees.

Scrub your potatoes well with a vegetable brush (leave the skins on) and pat them dry with a paper towel. Slice each potato in two lengthwise. Then slice each half lengthwise into two or three wedges, depending on the size of the spud.

Put a very small amount of vegetable oil—no more than a teaspoonful for up to four large potatoes—into a plastic bag. Put the potato wedges into the bag and shake well so that each wedge has a light, thin coating of oil.

Spread the wedges on a cookie sheet and sprinkle them lightly with your choice of seasonings. Some people stick with pepper and a little bit of salt, but you might want to experiment with chili powder, curry powder, paprika, garlic salt, or herbs such as dill and rosemary. Just remember, a little seasoning goes a long way.

Now bake your jo-jos in the oven for about forty minutes or until they are golden brown and crispy on the outside. Turn them once or twice while baking so that they cook evenly. Let them cool a bit, and enjoy a bite of Idaho!

Livestock ranching accounts for about a third of Idaho's agricultural income. The state's land and climate are well suited to sheep. Idahoans also raise both beef and dairy cattle. Several large hatcheries in Idaho produce trout to stock the state's rivers and to sell. Idaho is the country's top trout producer. If you order trout in a restaurant, chances are it came from an Idaho hatchery.

## TIMBER AND MINING

Idaho's mining and timber industries suffered in the 1980s and early 1990s, when demand for their minerals and wood products fell. Prices dropped, and many people lost their jobs. Some timber companies went out of business. Most companies that survived did so by streamlining and modernizing—in other words, by employing fewer people. Many mines also closed. This led to high unemployment in the mining districts of the north.

Today, the mining industry employs only about 3,100 Idahoans. "You hear a lot of talk about moving people into new jobs for the future," a thirty-nine-year-old Kellogg man said bitterly after losing his job. "You can't tell me someone's going to teach me to be a computer programmer, when all I've ever done is work in the mines." Some aspects of Idaho's economy may be booming, but hard times are still a reality in communities that have long depended on a single industry.

*A miner installs rock bolts for roof support at a silver mine near Wallace.*

# EARNING A LIVING

**Manufacturing**

Computers

Food processing

Wood processing

**Agriculture**

Barley

Cattle

Potatoes

Sheep

Sugar beets

Wheat

**Natural Resources**

G  Gold

Sand and Gravel

S  Silver

Timber

Priest Lake

Sandpoint

Lake Pend Oreille

Coeur d'Alene

Coeur d'Alene Lake

St. Joe R.

Elk River

Moscow

Lewiston

Snake R.

Duworshak Reservoir

Selway R.

Grangeville

Salmon R.

Warren

South Fork

Middle Fork

Salmon

Salmon R.

Island Park Reservoir

Snake R.

Cascade Reservoir

Payette R.

Weiser

Payette

Ashton

Rexburg

Caldwell

Meridian

Nampa

Boise

Ketchum

Idaho Falls

Palisades Reservoir

Blackfoot

Snake R.

Mountain Home

American Falls Reservoir

Pocatello

Blackfoot Reservoir

Snake R.

American Falls

Bruneau R.

Bear R.

Montpelier

Twin Falls

Goose Cr.

Burley

Bear Lake

Owyhee R.

Despite economic ups and downs, lumber production remains Idaho's fifth-ranking industry in terms of income, while mining ranks sixth. The state's mines produce significant amounts of lead, silver, phosphate, and other minerals. Idaho is called the Gem State, not just because of the phony "gem of the mountains" name. Many gems have been mined in Idaho. The most commercially important is the garnet, a deep red stone. Idaho's state stone is the star garnet, a special kind of garnet more valuable than either rubies or sapphires. There's also gold in the Idaho hills. Some is mined commercially. Some is teased out of riverbanks and hillsides by individual prospectors who have staked claims much like those of the long-ago gold rush.

*Logs await processing at a Coeur d'Alene sawmill.*

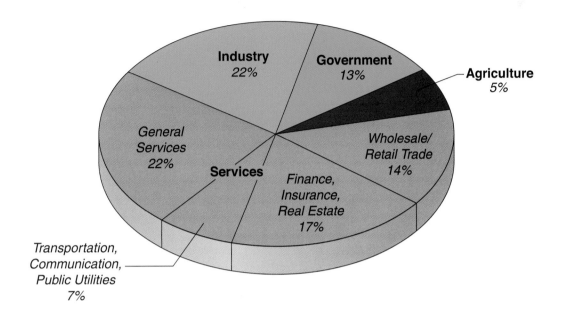

**2006 GROSS STATE PRODUCT: $50 Million**

Industry 22%

Government 13%

Agriculture 5%

General Services 22%

Services

Finance, Insurance, Real Estate 17%

Wholesale/ Retail Trade 14%

Transportation, Communication, Public Utilities 7%

## TRADING ACROSS THE BORDER

Canada, Idaho's neighbor to the north, is also one of the state's important trade partners. In 2004, Idaho sold $399 million in goods to Canada. (The only country that bought more goods from Idaho was the United Kingdom.) Idaho's leading exports were fertilizer, computers, medicines and chemicals, and electronics parts. In the same year, Idaho imported $534 million in goods from Canada. These imports included lumber, oil and coal products, fertilizer, vegetables, and animal feed. Idaho also imports wood pulp, plastics, engines and engine parts, and shipping containers.

Canada and Idaho are connected in other ways besides trade. Tourism crosses the Canada-Idaho border in both directions. In 2004, visitors from Canada spent $34 million in Idaho, while Idahoans spent about the same amount in Canada. Several of Idaho's employers, such as McCain Foods and

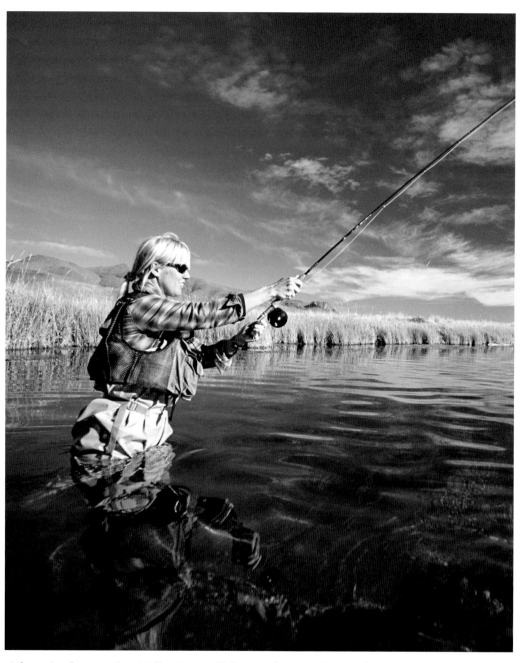

*Silver Creek, near Sun Valley, is a well-known location for catching prize-winning trout.*

Circle K Stores, are Canadian-owned companies. Boise State University has introduced a Canadian studies program that gives Idaho students a chance to explore Canada's trade, border, and environmental issues.

## CATCHING THE TOURIST DOLLAR

These days a different kind of gold rush is happening along Idaho's streams and in its mountains. People are coming to Idaho in ever-increasing numbers to fish, to hike, to camp, to run white-water rapids, to rock climb, to ski, and to mountain bike. Tourism and travel is the state's third-largest industry. The sport-fishing industry alone brings more than $100 million to Idaho each year as fishers spend money on gas, food, lodging, bait, tackle, guide services, boat rentals, and fishing and boating permits.

From vacationing families to retirees cruising the scenic byways in recreational vehicles to hard-core, no-frills backpackers, Idaho seems to have something for everyone. Hiker Dean Bethea reported that a three-day hike around the Seven Devils Range featured magnificent views, challenging climbs, and a brisk swim in a mountain lake. He left "tired, exhilarated, and convinced that the Northwest has few ranges that compare with the Seven Devils when it comes to scenery and the variety of trails."

What draws people to Idaho? And why do so many come back again and again? Larry EchoHawk, a man of mixed white and Native American descent who has served as the state attorney general and has been a candidate for governor, thinks he has the answer: "Idaho is what America once was, and what the rest of the nation now wants to be."

## Chapter Six

# Gem State Road Trip

Idaho has many treasures that can be discovered on a road trip from north to south. "Watch out," one resident warned a visitor. "You might like it so much you'll never get out."

### NORTHERN IDAHO

The Idaho Panhandle has the West's largest concentration of lakes. It's a wonderland for kayakers and canoeists. Golfers face an unusual challenge at the Coeur d'Alene Resort's course. Part of the course is located on an island in Lake Coeur d'Alene, and players must ride a boat out to play it.

East of the lake is the Silver Valley, a scene of mining history. The entire town of Wallace, called the Silver Capital of the World, has been registered as a National Historic Place. At the Sierra Silver Mine, you can hop aboard a trolley that will take you for a seventy-five-minute tour through the tunnels. You'll see mining equipment in operation, discover what silver ore looks like (it's not always silver), and learn how miners get the earth to give up its treasures.

*Mountain bikers and other adventurers are drawn to Idaho's steep, twisting forest trails and spectacular scenery.*

# PLACES TO SEE

*Kaniksu National Forest*

*Priest Lake*

Sandpoint

*Lake Pend Oreille*

*Coeur d'Alene National Forest*

Coeur d'Alene

*Coeur d'Alene Lake*

*St. Joe R.*

*Sierra Silver Mine*

*Old Mission State Park*

*St. Joe National Forest*

*St. Joe National Forest*

Elk River

Moscow

*Cleawater National Forest*

Lewiston

*Dworshak Reservoir*

*Snake R.*

*Selway R.*

Grangeville

*Nez Perce National Historic Park*

*Salmon R.*

*Hells Canyon National Recreation Area*

Warren

*South Fork*

*Frank Church River of No Return Wilderness*

Salmon

*Salmon National Forest*

*Middle Fork*

*Salmon R.*

*Ponderosa State Park*

*Boise National Forest*

*Snake R.*

*Payette R.*

*Salmon National Forest*

*Island Park Reservoir*

*Targhee National Forest*

▲ *Borah Peak (12,662 ft.)*

Weiser

Payette

Ashton

Rexburg

Caldwell   Meridian

*Capitol*

*Sun Valley*

*Targhee National Forest*

Nampa   Boise

Ketchum

*Craters of the Moon National Monument*

Idaho Falls

*Boise Art Museum*

*Discovery Center of Idaho*

*Palisades Reservoir*

Mountain Home

*Snake R.*

Blackfoot
*Fort Hall*

*Caribou National Forest*

*Silver City*

*Snake R.*

*American Falls Reservoir*

*Blackfoot Reservoir*

*Hagerman Fossil Beds*

*Shoshone Falls*

American Falls

Pocatello

*Lava Hot Springs*

*Bear R.*

Twin Falls

Burley

*Bruneau R.*

*Goose Cr.*

*Sawtooth National Forest*

*City of Rocks National Reserve*

Montpelier

*Caribou National Forest*

*Cache National Forest*

*Bear Lake*

*Ouyhee R.*

N
W   E
S

Farther south is Lewiston. As you gaze across the Snake River at the rolling wheat fields of Washington State stretching away as far as the eye can see, you might not realize that Lewiston is a Pacific Ocean port. Thanks to channel dredging and locks around several dams, oceangoing vessels can travel 470 miles from the mouth of the Columbia River to Lewiston to take on cargoes of grain, timber, and potatoes. While you are in the area, visit the Nez Perce National Historical Park and Museum, which has a fine collection of Nez Perce artifacts. Not far away is Spalding, named for Idaho's early missionary. The Saint Joseph's Mission, built in 1874, still stands nearby.

## CENTRAL IDAHO

Lewiston and the town of Riggins to the south are gateways to the extraordinary world of Hells Canyon. At its deepest point the canyon measures 8,000 feet from mountain peak to surging water—deeper than the Grand Canyon. Although there are gravel roads into the Hells Canyon National Recreation Area, the best way to see the canyon is by hiking along the rim or taking a boat on the river. Several outfitters offer paddleboat and powerboat trips through the canyon.

The glory of north-central Idaho is the great River of No Return. If you arrange a white-water trip on the Salmon River, you'll float or paddle past Native American petroglyphs (carvings on cliff walls), abandoned mine workings, and isolated ranches tucked into the hills. You might also experience a cold dunking when your boat flips over in a rapid, so be sure to wear a life preserver!

*Hells Canyon, on the Idaho-Oregon border, is a rugged stretch of the Pacific Northwest.*

Except for the roads that snake through the Clearwater Valley in the west, central Idaho is largely roadless. An exception is Highway 12, which roughly follows the route of Lewis and Clark across Idaho. A drive along this highway will introduce you to the Lochsa River, which has been designated a National Wild and Scenic River, and to a magnificent stretch of national forest dotted with hot springs and trailheads. At the eastern border of Idaho the road crosses Lolo Pass where Lewis and Clark did.

If your vehicle is sturdy, you may try venturing onto some of the twisting, rutted forest roads that wind into valleys and along ridges. Soon, however, those roads peter out and there's nothing but roadless wilderness in front of you. Some wilderness explorers claim that Idaho offers some of the finest hiking in the world. "Backpacking in the Bitterroots is the experience of a lifetime," claims Brenda Charris of Oregon. "It was like being alone in a perfect world before people arrived on the scene."

## SOUTHERN IDAHO

Southern Idaho has the largest share of the state's city lights. In Boise, the capitol building is not to be missed. This lovely domed structure is patterned after the United States Capitol in Washington, D.C., but has some distinctively Idahoan touches. For example, Idaho's capitol is heated by water from a geothermal well, an increasingly popular energy source in a state filled with hot springs and steam vents. In addition, the impressive statue of George Washington on horseback is not made of marble or bronze. An Austrian immigrant named Charles Ostner carved the statue from a massive yellow pine. He had only a picture of Washington on a postage stamp to serve as a model.

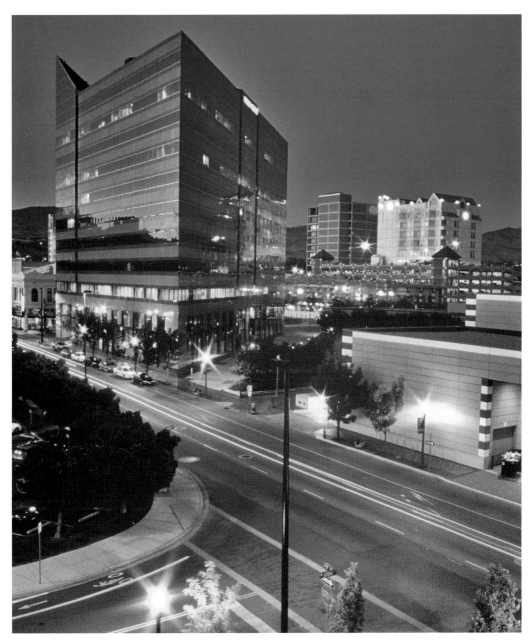

*Idaho's urban life is concentrated in Boise, although nearby communities such as Nampa are growing fast.*

## TEN LARGEST CITIES

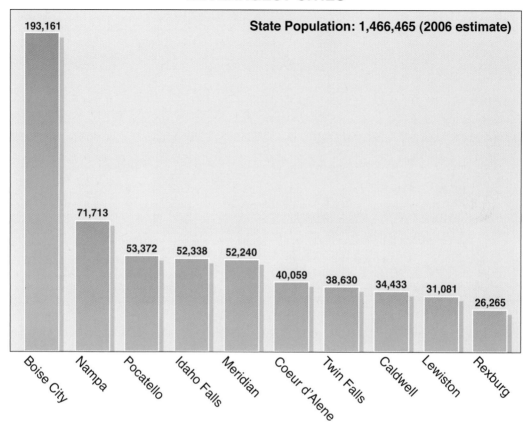

State Population: 1,466,465 (2006 estimate)

| City | Population |
|------|------------|
| Boise City | 193,161 |
| Nampa | 71,713 |
| Pocatello | 53,372 |
| Idaho Falls | 52,338 |
| Meridian | 52,240 |
| Coeur d'Alene | 40,059 |
| Twin Falls | 38,630 |
| Caldwell | 34,433 |
| Lewiston | 31,081 |
| Rexburg | 26,265 |

A good way to see Boise's historic and downtown neighborhoods is from the tour train, which provides a one-hour narrated ride through the city. If you'd rather explore on your own, Boise is a comfortable walking city, with coffee shops on many corners, café tables on sidewalks during mild weather, and plenty of shade trees. The city's name means "wooded" in French. French-Canadian trappers suggested the name because they were grateful for the shade trees along the Boise River in the otherwise sunbaked landscape of the Snake River Plain.

Relics of Idaho's history dot the southwestern part of the state. Silver City in the Owyhee Mountains is the Queen of Idaho Ghost Towns. This community formed after miners struck gold and silver in the 1860s and then faded away after the 1920s. A few people still live in Silver City, but the old drugstore and schoolhouse are now museums. Silver City is well worth a trip, but only in good weather—the 23-mile dirt road can be treacherous. Easier to reach is Idaho City, north of Boise. For a time during the gold rush of the 1860s, it was the biggest community in the Northwest. Boardwalks and buildings from that era survive. Many of the colorful structures now house modern businesses.

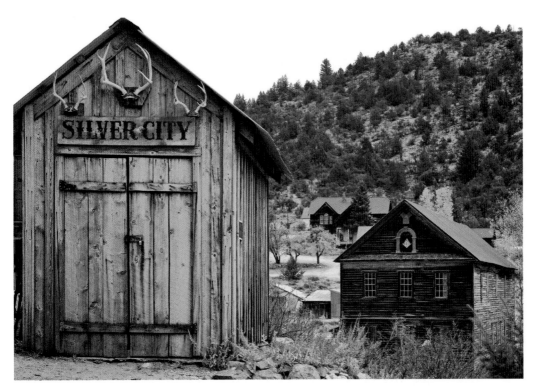

*The Queen of Idaho Ghost Towns, Silver City, is a relic of the mining boom's glory days.*

Southern Idaho has many unusual geological and geographic features. The Bruneau Dunes are a cluster of sand dunes that rise nearly 500 feet above the plain. Fossils of many creatures that once roamed this part of North America, including ancient horses, mastodons, and saber-toothed cats, have been found at Hagerman Fossil Beds. Just outside the town of Twin Falls is Shoshone Falls, a waterfall higher than New York's famed Niagara Falls. In spring, when the Snake River is at its highest, torrents of foam plunge 212 feet to a turbulent pool below. To the southeast, near Oakley, is the City of Rocks National Reserve. Early pioneers who wandered into this area were awestruck. Out of the rolling sagebrush landscape loom sixty-story granite columns that look like ghostly, silent skyscrapers.

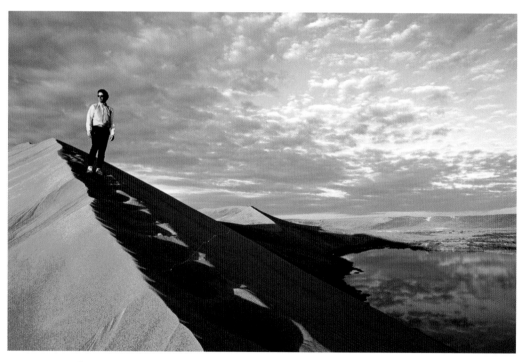

*From atop the Bruneau Sand Dunes, a hiker can gaze over the wide expanse of south-western Idaho.*

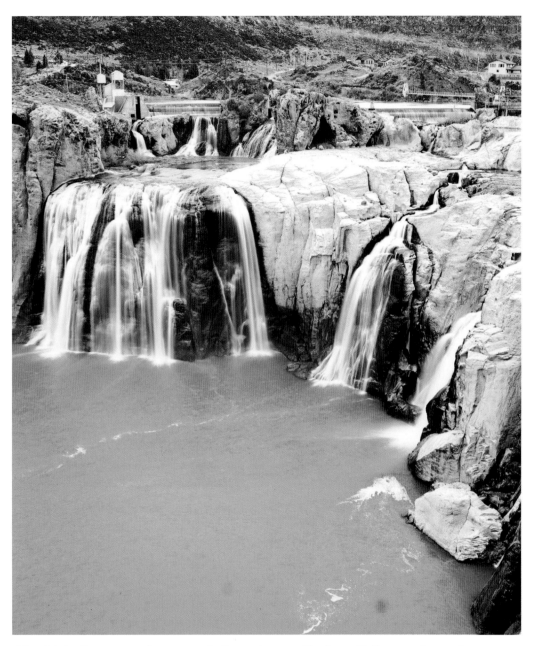

*The Snake River cascades over rock formations at Shoshone Falls near the southern Idaho city of Twin Falls.*

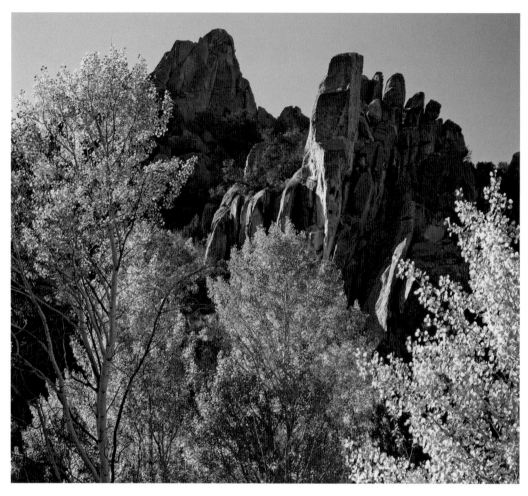

*The City of Rocks rises above a stand of quaking aspens, whose leaves paint the landscape with color in the fall.*

North of Twin Falls lies Sun Valley, where you may spot movie stars sharing the ski slopes with tanned teenage snowboarders. Sun Valley, along with the nearby towns of Hailey and Ketchum, is Idaho's center of glittering celebrity life. The surrounding area is home to ordinary, hardworking folks as well.

Eastern Idaho offers vistas of the magnificent spires of the Grand Tetons. One Twin Falls resident recalled showing a photograph of the Tetons to someone back east years ago. "That's a painting," the New Yorker scoffed. "There aren't really any mountains that are pointed like that."

Southeastern Idaho may not have sky-piercing crags or mile-deep canyons, but it has gentle charms of its own, with many scenic byways cutting through green hills. Bear Lake is a tranquil fishing and boating spot. Lava Hot Springs, with pools heated by the earth's volcanic forces, was once a camp shared by Shoshone and Bannock Indians. Today it has a resort with an Olympic-sized pool, tennis courts, and a golf course.

*In the shadow of the majestic Grand Tetons, a farmer in Fremont County harvests barley.*

## IDAHO'S MOONSCAPE

One early visitor called it "a desolate and awful waste." Another wrote that it was "the strangest 75 square miles on the North American continent." They were describing a place in southeastern Idaho where the land's volcanic past is visible on its tortured surface—an area covered with the black, crumbling remains of past lava flows.

The Shoshone never lived in this region, but they traveled over it. Pioneers gave it a wide berth—water was hard to find in the sunbaked black lava wastes, and the sharp rock would cut their animals' feet to ribbons. Settlers and ranchers considered the lava wasteland worthless. In 1924, however, Congress recognized its geological value and named it Craters of the Moon National Monument. Today it is one of the state's major tourist attractions. Drivers and bicyclists can follow a 7-mile loop past lava tubes, cones, caves, and other dramatic features.

At first glance the huge expanse of twisted, ribbed lava may seem as barren as the Moon. But look more closely. A swift, striped ground squirrel is scooting between two rocks. Overhead a prairie falcon soars lazily, and nearby a songbird pipes from a sunny ledge. In spring, Craters of the Moon blooms with short-lived but dazzling wildflowers. A different kind of life blooms there in midwinter, when brightly clad cross-country skiers glide along snow-covered trails through the lava wilderness.

As you explore southeastern Idaho you'll also find Soda Springs, where hot mineral water gushes forth from thirty springs. Pioneers called one of them Beer Springs. Its water doesn't taste much like beer, but the pioneers had been on the trail for a long, thirsty time. The Oregon Trail ran through Soda Springs, and foot-deep wagon ruts can still be seen on the local golf course. End your tour of Idaho where the pioneers used to begin it. As his wagon train approached Soda Springs, one settler wrote, "Here we enter the Snake countrie."

*Soda Springs is the only captive geyser in the world.*

THE FLAG: *The flag shows the state seal against a blue background. Below the seal is a scroll that reads "STATE OF IDAHO." Idaho's flag was first adopted in 1907 and readopted in 1957.*

THE SEAL: *The woman holding scales in Idaho's state seal symbolizes liberty, justice, and equality. The miner represents the state's mineral wealth, the elk's head stands for its wildlife, the pine tree for its forest, and the grain for its agriculture. The seal was originally adopted in 1891 and was readopted in 1957.*

# State Survey

**Statehood:** July 3, 1890

**Origin of Name:** A miner made up the name *Idaho*. He claimed it was a Native-American word meaning "gem of the mountains."

**Nickname:** Gem State

**Capital:** Boise

**Motto:** Let It Be Perpetual

**Bird:** mountain bluebird

**Flower:** syringa

**Tree:** Western white pine

**Gem:** star garnet

**Horse:** Appaloosa

**Folk Dance:** square dance

**Fish:** cutthroat trout

**Fossil:** Hagerman horse fossil

*Mountain bluebird*

*Syringa*

# HERE WE HAVE IDAHO

The music for the Idaho state song was composed in 1915 under the title "Garden of Paradise." In 1917, McKinley Helm, a student at the University of Idaho, wrote lyrics to it, and it was adopted as the university's song. In 1931, with a revised set of lyrics, the song was recognized as the official state song. It is also known as "Our Idaho."

**Words by Bethel Packenham and McKinley Helm**     **Music by Sallie Hume-Douglas**

You've heard of the won - ders our land does pos - sess, Its beau - ti - ful val - leys and hills;___ The ma - jest - ic for - est where na - ture a - bounds, We love ev - 'ry rock___ and rill.___ And here we have I - da - ho,___ Win - ning her way to fame.___ Sil - ver and gold in the sun - light blaze, And ro - mance lies in her name.___ Sing - ing, we're sing - ing of you, Ah, proud - ly, too; All our lives thro', we'll go Sing - ing, sing - ing of you, Sing - ing of I - da - ho.___

## GEOGRAPHY

**Highest Point:** 12,662 feet above sea level, at Mount Borah

**Lowest Point:** 710 feet, in Lewiston

**Area:** 83,574 square miles

**Greatest Distance North to South:** 483 miles

**Greatest Distance East to West:** 316 miles

**Bordering States:** Oregon and Washington to the west, Montana and Wyoming to the east, Nevada and Utah to the south

**Hottest Recorded Temperature:** 118 degrees Fahrenheit at Orofino on July 28, 1934

**Coldest Recorded Temperature:** –60 °F at Island Park Dam on January 18, 1943

**Average Annual Precipitation:** 19 inches

**Major Rivers:** Big Wood, Blackfoot, Boise, Bruneau, Clearwater, Payette, Pend Oreille, St. Joe, Salmon, Snake, Spokane, Weiser

**Major Lakes:** Alturas, Bear, Coeur d'Alene, Grays, Hayden, Henrys, Payette, Pend Oreille, Pettit, Priest, Redfish, Stanley

**Trees:** birch, cottonwood, Douglas fir, Engelmann spruce, hemlock, lodgepole pine, ponderosa pine, quaking aspen, western larch, western red cedar, white fir

**Wild Plants:** buttercup, columbine, elderberry, fireweed, huckleberry, larkspur, ocean spray, purple heather, thimbleberry, violet

**Animals:** beaver, black bear, bobcat, cougar, coyote, elk, mink, moose, mountain goat, otter, porcupine, prairie dog, pronghorn, raccoon, Rocky Mountain sheep, white-tailed deer

**Birds:** duck, eagle, falcon, goose, hawk, heron, meadowlark, partridge, pheasant, sandhill crane

**Fish:** bass, catfish, crappie, cutthroat trout, kamloops trout, perch, salmon, steelhead trout, sturgeon

**Endangered Animals:** American peregrine falcon, Banbury Springs limpet, Bliss Rapids snail, Bruneau hot springsnail, bull trout, gray wolf, grizzly bear, Idaho springsnail, Snake River physa snail, Utah valvata snail, white sturgeon, whooping crane, woodland caribou

**Endangered Plants:** MacFarlane's four-o'clock, Ute ladies'-tresses, water howellia

## TIMELINE

**Idaho History**

**1700s** Shoshone, Nez Perce, Bannock, Paiute, Coeur d'Alene, Kutenai, and Kalispell Indians live in present-day Idaho.

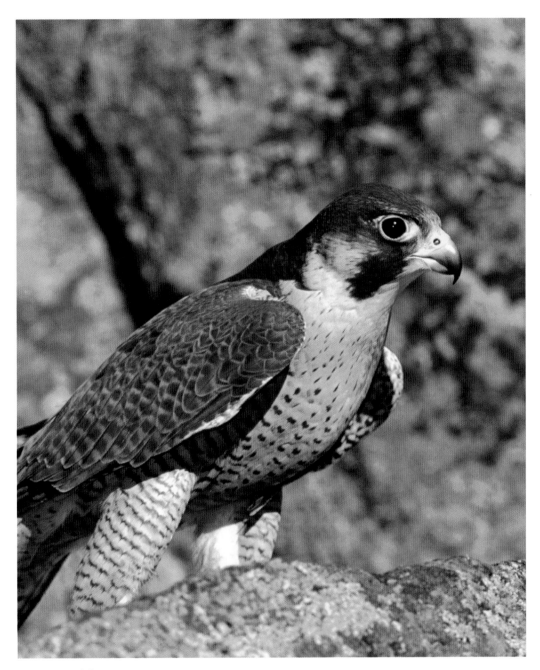

*Peregrine falcon*

**1805–1806** Lewis and Clark cross Idaho.

**1809** David Thompson builds a trading post near Lake Pend Oreille. This is the first non-Indian structure in Idaho.

**1832** The largest fur-trapper rendezvous ever is held at Pierre's Hole.

**1836** Henry and Eliza Spalding establish the region's first mission near present-day Lewiston.

**1842** The first pioneers pass through Idaho on the Oregon Trail.

**1850** Construction is completed on the Cataldo mission, the oldest standing structure in Idaho.

**1855** The first Mormons arrive in Idaho.

**1860** Franklin, Idaho's first permanent white settlement, is founded; gold is discovered on Orofino Creek.

**1862** The *Golden Age*, Idaho's first newspaper, begins publication in Lewiston.

**1863** The Idaho Territory is created; U.S. troops kill 368 Shoshone at the Battle of Bear River, the worst slaughter of Native Americans in U.S. history.

**1874** The Utah Northern Railroad enters Idaho.

**1877** U.S. troops force Chief Joseph and other Nez Perce Indians to submit to reservation life.

**1883** The Northern Pacific Railroad completes its line across northern Idaho.

**1884** One of the world's richest silver deposits is discovered in the Coeur d'Alene Mountains; the Union Pacific Railroad completes its line through southern Idaho.

**1889** The University of Idaho is founded in Moscow.

**1892** Violent labor struggles erupt in the mining region near Coeur d'Alene.

**1899** Governor Frank Steunenberg calls in federal troops to break a mining strike.

**1901** The Academy of Idaho—later Idaho State University—is founded.

**1905** Former governor Frank Steunenberg is murdered.

**1910** Forest fires in northern Idaho rage across 3 million acres.

**1914** Idahoans elect Moses Alexander, who becomes the nation's first Jewish governor.

**1938** Sun Valley, the first ski resort in the United States, opens.

**1942** Japanese Americans from the West Coast are sent to Camp Minidoka, near Twin Falls, for the rest of World War II.

**1951** Electricity is generated from nuclear energy for the first time at a testing station near Idaho Falls.

**1955** Arco becomes the world's first city to receive its power from nuclear energy.

**1972** Ninety-one miners die in a fire at the Sunshine Silver Mine near Wardner.

**1974** Kutenai Indians demand and receive a reservation.

**1975** Work is completed on the Columbia-Snake River Inland Waterway; Lewiston becomes the West's farthest-inland seaport.

**1988** Idaho voters approve a state lottery.

**1992** A siege at Ruby Ridge in northern Idaho results in several deaths and draws international attention to the tensions between federal law enforcement and Idahoans who defy the government.

**2000** Severe wildfires burn more than half a million acres of Idaho public forest.

**2001** A U.S. Supreme Court decision gives control of part of Lake Coeur d'Alene to the Coeur d'Alene tribe.

**2006** An agricultural pest called the potato cyst nematode is found in the United States for the first time in southern Idaho.

## ECONOMY

**Agricultural Products:** barley, beef cattle, dairy products, hay, hops, lentils, mint, onions, peas, plums, potatoes, sheep, sugar beets, wheat

**Manufactured Products:** chemicals, computers, electrical equipment, food products, lumber and wood products, metal products

**Natural Resources:** clay, copper, garnet, gold, lead, phosphate, sand and gravel, silver, timber

**Business and Trade:** finance, real estate, shipping, tourism, wholesale and retail trade

## CALENDAR OF CELEBRATIONS

**McCall Winter Carnival** McCall warms up during the dead of winter in late January and early February with a carnival that features ice sculptures, snowmobile races, parades, sleigh rides, and sled-dog contests.

*A potato mascot at the McCall Winter Carnival*

**Lionel Hampton Jazz Festival** Each February, this prestigious event in Moscow features both performances and workshops by fifty world-renowned jazz musicians. Past performers have included Wynton Marsalis, Ella Fitzgerald, and, of course, Lionel Hampton.

**Dodge National Circuit Finals Rodeo** Watch the dirt fly in Pocatello in March when the best cowboys and cowgirls from around the country compete in such events as broncobusting and calf roping at one of the nation's largest rodeos.

**Race to Robie Creek** Each April thousands of people push themselves to the limit at one of the nation's most grueling races, a thirteen-mile run up and over Aldape Summit in Boise.

**Western Days** Twin Falls celebrates its rough-and-tumble past at this late spring event that includes a staged shootout, a chili cook-off, a barbecue, dances, and a parade.

**Mountain Man Rendezvous** The rugged life of the mountain man is honored in American Falls in early June. Tepees, traders, and old-fashioned weapons are all part of this rendezvous, where participants try to re-create the mountain man's life as accurately as possible.

**National Oldtime Fiddlers' Contest** It's impossible to sit still when the best fiddlers from around the country converge on Weiser each June. This weeklong celebration features hundreds of fiddlers competing in contests and playing at jam sessions and dances. Apart from all the music, the event also includes parades, a golf tournament, and a barbecue.

**Teton Valley Hot Air Balloon Festival** Few events are as breathtakingly beautiful as this July festival in Driggs, where brightly colored hot air balloons race against a backdrop of the stunning spires of the Grand Teton Mountains. Balloon and glider rides, parades, and rodeos are all part of the fun.

**Festival of San Inazio** Boise's Basque community celebrates its heritage at this event that features traditional food, dancing, and contests of strength. It falls on the weekend closest to July 31, the birth date of Saint Inazio.

**Snake River Stampede** One of the West's largest horse parades and a lavish breakfast kick off this July rodeo in Nampa.

**Payette Whitewater Roundup** Champion kayakers from all over the world come to Banks each July to compete in the world's soggiest "rodeo." These white-water experts race, surf, and perform tricks on the Payette River rapids.

**Idaho International Folk Dance Festival** Dancers from as far away as India, Malaysia, and Russia descend on Rexburg in late July and early August for this event. In addition to watching magnificent dancing, you can also enjoy a rodeo and country music, which give international visitors a taste of American folk culture.

**Shoshone-Bannock Indian Festival and Rodeo** Each August, Fort Hall hosts one of the biggest powwows in the West. Native Americans and non-Indians alike enjoy the dancing, drumming, arts and crafts, rodeo, and softball tournament.

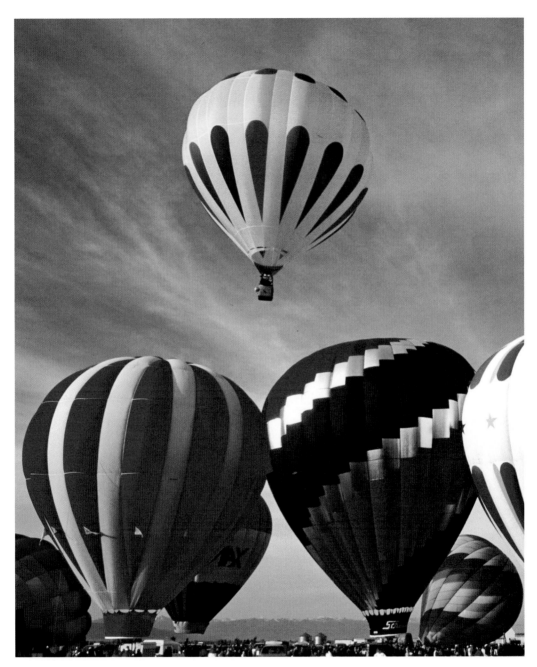

*The Teton Valley Hot Air Balloon Festival*

**Three Island Crossing Reenactment** The drama and danger of
traveling the Oregon Trail is re-created each August in Glenns
Ferry. Oxen, wagons, and people dressed as pioneers splash, swim,
and struggle across the Snake River at a spot where many
pioneers crossed it.

*Reenacting a historic pioneer crossing of the Snake River at Three Island Crossing State Park*

**Idaho Spud Day** Shelly celebrates Idaho's "famous potatoes" in September when thousands of Idahoans gather to compete in potato picking and peeling competitions. During the festival, you can watch a big parade while enjoying your spuds baked, fried, mashed, or scalloped.

**Art in the Park** Each September, hundreds of artists display their work at this three-day event, which attracts 150,000 visitors to Boise.

**Sun Valley Swing 'n' Dixie Jazz Jamboree** Each October in Sun Valley, two dozen swing, ragtime, and traditional jazz bands provide the music for five great days of dancing and fun.

**Cottages and Cranberries Festival** Get into the holiday spirit early at this event in Pocatello's quaint old town. You can enjoy horse-drawn carriage rides, listen to carolers, and admire elaborate gingerbread houses and old-fashioned crafts.

## STATE STARS

**Joe Albertson** (1906–1993) founded the Albertson's chain of grocery stores. When Albertson opened his first store in Boise in 1939, he made it larger than other grocery stores and included a butcher, a bakery, and an ice cream parlor. This was the first supermarket. Today, Albertson's is one of the nation's largest grocery chains. Albertson grew up in Caldwell.

**William Edgar Borah** (1865–1940) was a senator who earned the nickname Lion of Idaho for his strong devotion to principles and his forceful speeches. After working as an attorney in Boise, Borah was elected to the U.S. Senate in 1906. As an isolationist, Borah felt that the United States should avoid getting entangled in foreign affairs. In 1919, when President Woodrow Wilson wanted the United States to join the League of Nations, Borah became famous by touring the country and making speeches against the league. In the end, the United States did not join. Later, Borah helped create the U.S. Department of Labor. In 1936 he became the first Idahoan to run for president, but he did not earn the Republican nomination. Borah continued to serve in the Senate until his death.

**Gutzon Borglum** (1867–1941) was the artist who carved Mount Rushmore. Borglum, who was born in Bear Lake, was already noted for his enormous sculptures of animals and frontier life when he began work on Mount Rushmore in 1927. He continued his work sculpting the faces of George Washington, Abraham Lincoln, Thomas Jefferson, and Theodore Roosevelt into the side of a mountain in South Dakota until his death.

**Carol Ryrie Brink** (1895–1981) wrote books for both adults and children. In 1936, she won the Newbery Medal, honoring the year's best children's novel, for *Caddie Woodlawn*, which was based on stories she had heard from her pioneer grandmother. Her novels, many of which were set near her hometown of Moscow, have a strong sense of place and a lively spirit of adventure.

*Gutzon Borglum*

**Edgar Rice Burroughs** (1875–1950) created the character Tarzan, a man who was raised by apes in Africa. Burroughs began writing Tarzan adventures in 1912. He eventually wrote twenty-six Tarzan books, and the character was featured in many movies and television programs. Burroughs grew up in Chicago but spent many summers in Idaho, where his brothers had a ranch. Later, Burroughs himself lived in Idaho on and off.

**Frank Church** (1924–1984) of Boise was a U.S. senator for twenty-four years. In 1956, at age thirty-two, he became the fifth-youngest member of the Senate. He is perhaps best remembered for his efforts to conserve wilderness areas in Idaho. The Frank Church River of No Return Wilderness Area is named in his honor.

**Philo Farnsworth** (1906–1971) was an inventor known as the Father of Television. He put together the first television system, which he demonstrated in 1927. Farnsworth also invented the first simple electron microscope. He was born in Utah and grew up in Rigby, Idaho.

**Vardis Fisher** (1895–1968), a native of Annis, wrote novels that described the rough life on the American frontier. Some of his best-known works include *Mountain Man* and *The Children of God*.

**Emma Edwards Green** (1856–1942) designed Idaho's state seal. Green, who grew up in California, went to art school in New York. Passing through Boise on her way home, she fell in love with the city and decided to stay. She soon entered a competition to design

*Philo Farnsworth*

the seal of the new state and was the unanimous winner. This made her the only woman to design a state seal. She lived in Boise for the rest of her life.

**Ernest Hemingway** (1899–1961) was one of the most influential writers of the twentieth century. His direct, stripped-down prose was copied by seemingly every young writer of his time. Among Hemingway's best-known books are *The Sun Also Rises* and *The Old Man and the Sea*. In 1954, he won the Nobel Prize for literature, the world's most prestigious writing award. Born in Illinois, Hemingway was a frequent visitor to Sun Valley before finally settling in Ketchum for the last years of his life.

**Chief Joseph** (1840–1904) was a Nez Perce chief who led eight hundred people—mostly women, children, and old men—on an amazing retreat through Idaho and Montana in 1877. U.S. troops were trying to force Joseph's people from their homeland in northeastern Oregon to a reservation in Idaho. To avoid this, Joseph led his people on a 1,000-mile trek through the wilderness. He won many battles in Idaho along the way. U.S. troops eventually caught up with Chief Joseph in Montana near the Canadian border.

**Harmon Killebrew** (1936–    ), one of baseball's greatest home run hitters, was born in Payette. Playing for the Washington Senators and the Minneapolis Twins, he became famous for his incredible power, which sometimes sent balls all the way out of the stadium. With 573 home runs, Killebrew has the fifth-highest total in Major League Baseball. He was elected to the National Baseball Hall of Fame in 1984.

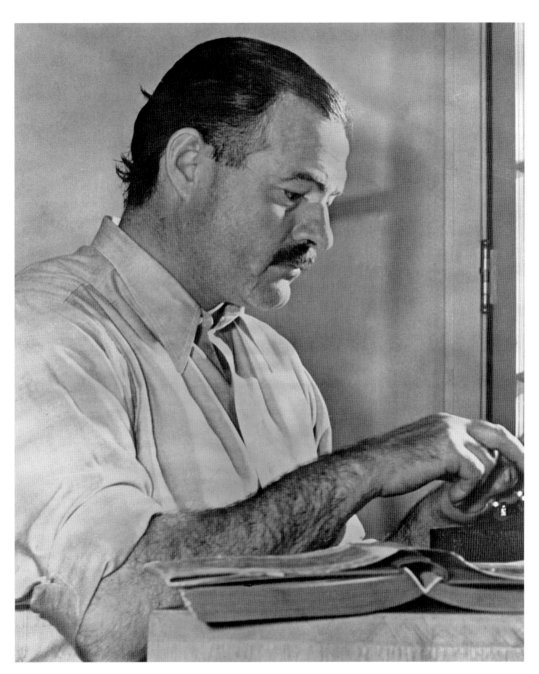

*Ernest Hemingway*

**Jerry Kramer** (1936–  ) was a leading football player of the 1960s. He began his professional career as a guard for the Green Bay Packers in 1958. Later, he also became the Packers' placekicker. By the time he retired in 1968, he had been named all-pro five times and had played on five championship teams. Kramer was born in Montana and grew up in Sandpoint, Idaho.

**Dan O'Brien** (1966–  ) holds the world record in the decathlon, a grueling two-day track and field contest in which athletes compete in ten different events. He won the gold medal in the decathlon at the 1996 Summer Olympics. O'Brien lives in Moscow.

**Ezra Pound** (1885–1972), one of the most influential poets of the twentieth century, was born in Hailey. Pound believed that poetry should play an important role in society. He spent much of his life writing a long series of poems called *Cantos*, which deals with such weighty issues as history and economics. Pound also edited several important literary journals and promoted the work of avant-garde writers.

**Sacagawea** (1784–1812?) was an interpreter on the Lewis and Clark expedition across the western United States. She was born in central Idaho into the Lemhi band of Shoshone. Sacagawea began traveling with Lewis and Clark in North Dakota and helped guide them peacefully through Shoshone territory. She was the only woman on the expedition. Along the way, she gave birth to the expedition's only child.

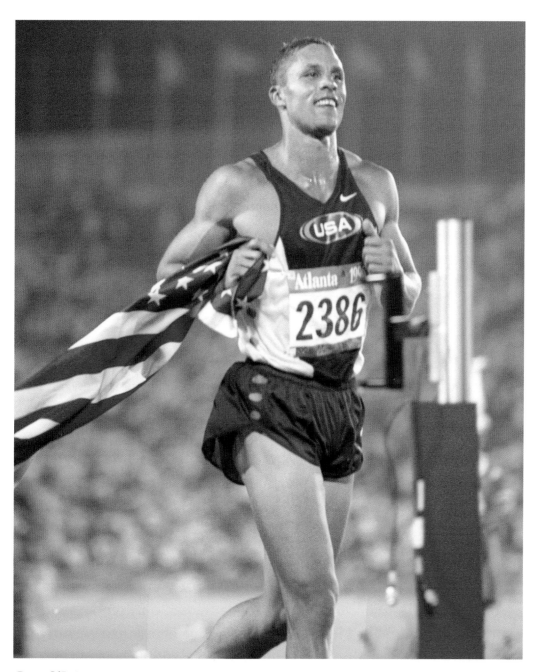

*Dan O'Brien*

**J. R. "Jack" Simplot** (1909–   ) turned a small potato farm into an empire and became one of the richest people in the United States. By 1941, Simplot was producing more potatoes than any other farmer in Idaho. He made his first million selling dried potatoes to the military. Today, his company supplies more than half of McDonald's french fries. His business is also involved in mining, frozen fruits and vegetables, and even computer parts.

**Henry Spalding** (1804–1874), a missionary, was the first permanent white settler in Idaho. In 1836, he and his wife, Eliza, founded the Lapwai Mission near present-day Lewiston. The mission included Idaho's first church, school, and sawmill.

**Picabo Street** (1971–   ), a champion skier, grew up in Triumph. Street was a national junior skiing champion as a teenager. In 1995, she became the first American woman to win the World Cup skiing title. She has won two Olympic medals, including a gold in the Super-G event in the 1998 Winter Olympics. Street's fearlessness and exuberant, playful personality are as famous as her skiing prowess.

**David Thompson** (1770–1857) was a Canadian explorer and fur trader. In 1809, while working for the North West Company, he constructed the first non-Indian structure in Idaho, a trading post on the shores of Lake Pend Oreille. He is also famous for being the first person to travel the entire length of the Columbia River and for making an important early map of northwestern North America.

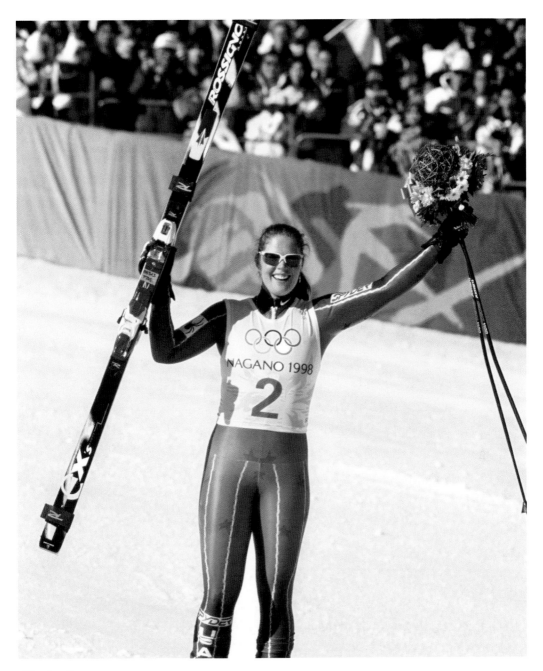

*Picabo Street*

**Lana Turner** (1920–1995), a popular movie star of the 1940s and 1950s, was known for her elegance and poise. Turner got her start in the movies as a teenager after she was discovered at a soda fountain in Los Angeles. She became famous for her performances in such melodramas as *The Postman Always Rings Twice* and *Imitation of Life*. Turner was born in Wallace.

*Lana Turner*

## TOUR THE STATE

**Frank Church River of No Return Wilderness** (Salmon) The nation's largest wilderness area outside of Alaska, this vast mountainous region covers an area larger than Rhode Island. It offers endless opportunities for hiking, white-water rafting, and wildlife watching. The wilderness also includes many soothing hot springs.

**Hells Canyon National Recreation Area** (Riggins) The best ways to experience Hells Canyon, the deepest river canyon in North America, are to hike along its rim or to raft on the Snake River, more than a mile below. The canyon offers a variety of sights, ranging from cacti to Native American rock drawings to bald eagles.

**Nez Perce National Historical Park** (Spalding) This park includes thirty-eight different sites from Nez Perce history, twenty-nine of which are in Idaho. The park headquarters is near the site of Lapwai Mission. Elsewhere the park preserves archaeological sites, battle sites, and geographic features important in Nez Perce mythology.

**Shoshone Falls** (Twin Falls) More than 200 feet tall and 1,000 feet wide, this horseshoe-shaped falls is most awe-inspiring in spring, when it is swollen with melted show.

**Fort Hall** (Pocatello) The reconstruction of one of the most important trading posts on the Oregon Trail brings history to life. In addition to active blacksmith and carpentry shops, there are exhibits about Native Americans, the Oregon Trail, and the fort's history.

**Sun Valley** The oldest, and one of the most lavish, ski resorts in the country offers great alpine skiing, fast lifts, and luxurious lodgings.

**City of Rocks National Reserve** (Almo) Huge spires of granite lure rock climbers from all over the world to this remote site. Nearby is Register Rock, where passing pioneers wrote their names.

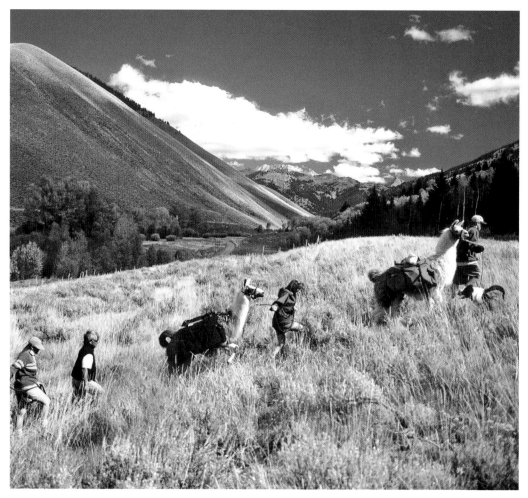

*Trekking in Sun Valley*

**Silver City** Hidden high in the Owyhee Mountains is Idaho's best-preserved ghost town. Walking the streets of Silver City gives you the feel of what life was like in the mad days of the late nineteenth-century silver boom.

**Harriman State Park** (Island Park) Henry's Fork River, which runs through the park, is one of the country's best fly-fishing spots. The park is also ideal for hiking, biking, horseback riding, cross-country skiing, and viewing trumpeter swans, sandhill cranes, elk, beavers, and other wildlife.

**Lava Hot Springs** (Lava Hot Springs) In a beautiful hollow overlooking the Portneuf River, these hot springs feed several pools that stay a soothing 102 °F.

**Ponderosa State Park** (McCall) Magnificent 400-year-old, 150-foot-tall Ponderosa pines tower over this park. Hiking, biking, and swimming are popular activities. There's even a lighted trail for nighttime cross-country skiing.

**Hagerman Fossil Beds National Monument** (Hagerman) This national monument is one of the world's principal fossil beds. Fossils of 140 species have been found here. Discoveries include more than 125 full skeletons of an ancient animal called the Hagerman horse, which is the state fossil.

**Discovery Center of Idaho** (Boise) A skeleton riding a bicycle is just one of the exhibits that makes science fun at this hands-on museum.

**World Center for Birds of Prey** (Boise) The center is dedicated to breeding endangered birds of prey such as peregrine falcons and releasing them into the wild. Visitors can watch presentations about birds of prey and get close-up views of injured birds.

**Boise Art Museum** (Boise) The pride of this beautiful museum is its collection of realist paintings. Some are so detailed that they almost look like photographs. At night, the museum often hosts jazz concerts and other events.

**Idaho Historical Museum** (Boise) You'll learn about the dramatic history of Idaho's Native Americans, fur traders, prospectors, and pioneers at this fascinating museum. Outside are some of Boise's earliest buildings.

**Basque Museum and Cultural Center** (Boise) Exhibits at the museum cover Basque history, both in Idaho and in the Basque homeland on the border between France and Spain. Displays include Basque crafts and musical instruments.

**Idaho's World Potato Exposition** (Blackfoot) This shrine to the pride of Idaho is filled with potato facts and memorabilia, including the world's largest potato chip.

**Paris Stake Tabernacle** (Paris) This majestic Mormon temple, made of red sandstone, was built in the 1880s.

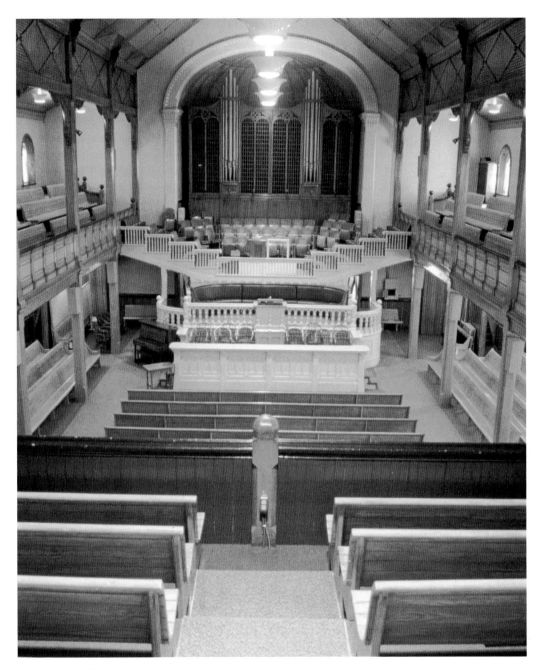

*Paris Stake Tabernacle*

**Craters of the Moon National Monument** (Arco) The twisted, contorted remains of lava flows from thousands of years ago make Craters of the Moon an eerie and fascinating place to explore.

**Old Mission State Park** (Cataldo) Construction was completed on the elegant Cataldo Mission, the oldest standing structure in Idaho, in 1853. The park features exhibits on the history of the mission and the Coeur d'Alene Indians, as well as interpretive trails.

**Sierra Silver Mine** (Wallace) Venturing into the depths of an old silver mine, you'll learn about the history and process of extracting the precious metal from the ground.

### FUN FACTS

The world's first alpine ski lift was built in 1938 in the new ski resort of Sun Valley. It cost twenty-five cents per ride.

Idaho's Big Wood River has a very strange claim to fame. One section of it is 4 feet wide and 100 feet deep, while a nearby section spreads to 100 feet wide and 4 feet deep.

The city of Island Park has the nation's longest Main Street. It stretches for almost 37 miles, passing by the string of resorts that make up most of the town.

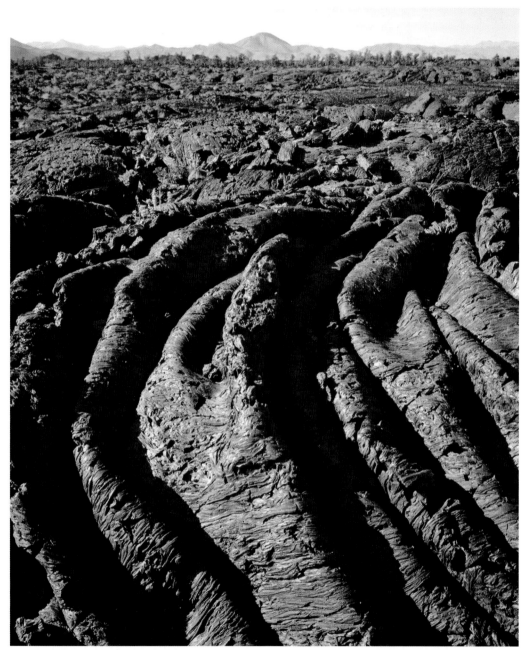

*Craters of the Moon National Monument*

# Find Out More

If you would like to find out more about Idaho, look in your school library, local library, bookstore, or video store. You can also surf the Internet. Here are some resources to help you begin your search.

### GENERAL STATE BOOKS

Edwards, Karen. *Idaho: The Gem State*. Strongsville, OH: World Almanac Library, 2003.

Hodgkins, Fran. *Idaho*. Mankato, MN: Capstone Press, 2003.

Miller, Amy. *Idaho*. New York: Children's Press, 2003.

### BOOKS ABOUT IDAHO PEOPLE, PLACES, AND HISTORY

Aiken, Katherine, Kevin R. Marsh, and Laura Woodworth-Ney. *Idaho: The Heroic Journey*. Encino, CA: Cherbo Publishing, 2006.

Marsh, Carole. *Idaho Indians*. Atlanta: Gallopade, 2004.

McGregor, Carol Lynn. *Lewis and Clark's Bittersweet Crossing*. Caldwell, ID: Caxton Press, 2004.

### DVDS AND VIDEOS

*Exploring Hell's Canyon: Jet Boating on the Snake River*. American Odyssey, n.d.

*Idaho Ghost Towns: A Journey Through Time*. Smede Marketing
   Productions, 2007.


## WEB SITES

### Idaho

www.state.id.us

Idaho's official state Web site includes state facts, government, education,
tourism, and more.


### Idaho Quick Facts

http://quickfacts.census.gov/qfd/states/16000.html

Information from the U.S. Census Bureau paints a numeric portrait of
Idaho's population, broken down by city, county, and ethnic group.


### Native Americans in Idaho

http://imnh.isu.edu/digitalatlas/geog/native/natvfr.htm

Part of the Digital Atlas of Idaho, this page offers information
about the history, ways of life, and influence of Idaho's various
native peoples.


### Digital Atlas of Idaho

http://imnh.isu.edu/digitalatlas/index.htm

Developed by a group of educational and cultural institutions,
including the Idaho Museum of Natural History and Idaho State
University, this well-designed site has information and links to
resources on Idaho's geology, geography, archaeology, history, climate,
wildlife, and more.

## Idaho State Historical Society

http://www.idahohistory.net/

This Web page offers an extensive timeline of Idaho history, an overview of historical sites, a "This Week in Idaho History" feature, and links to other museums and historical societies around the state.

## Ghost Towns of Idaho

http://www.ghosttowns.com/states/id/id.html

Idaho is dotted with dusty, fading ghost towns, most of them abandoned after mining booms. This site lists dozens of them by county, with brief histories and directions for visiting.

# Index

Page numbers in **boldface** are illustrations and charts.

agriculture, 23–24, 47, 80–84
Alexander, Moses, 70
Andrus, Cecil, 70, **70**
anthropology, 30
Appaloosa horses, 32, **32**
Apple Blossom Festival, 63
archaeology, 33
Arco, Idaho, 50
Arrowrock Dam, **25**
Aryan Nations, 51–52

Basque Museum and Cultural
  Center, 60
Bear Lake, 101
Beer Springs, 103
Big Lost River, 14
Bitterroot Mountains, 12, 37
Blue Spring Hills, 12
Boise, Idaho, 23, 44, 56, 67, 94,
  **95,** 96
Boise River, 27, **27**
borders and boundaries, 9, 11
Bridger, Jim, 38, **38**
Bruneau Dunes, 98, **98**
Butler, Richard, 51

Canada, 87
Candidate Conservation Agree-
  ments with Assurances (CCAAs),
  19–20
Caribou Mountains, 12
Central Idaho, 93–94
Cherry Festival, 63
City of Rocks National Reserve,
  98, **100**
Clark, William, **36,** 36–37, 94
Clearwater River, 14
Clearwater Valley, 94
Cleveland, Grover, 46
climate, 13–15
Coeur d'Alene, Idaho, 67

Coeur d'Alene Range, 12
Coeur d'Alene Resort, 91
Coeur d'Alene River, 14
Coeur d'Alene sawmill, **86**
colleges and universities, 64
Colter, John, 38
Columbia River, 12
conservation, 17–21, 22, 24,
  26–27, 53
Corps of Discovery, **36,** 36–37
cougar, **16**
cowgirl, **54**
Craters of the Moon National
  Monument, 102, **102**
crops, 47, 80–83, **81,** 85
culture, 61–64

dams, 24, **25,** 53
De Smet, Pierre Jean, 38, **39**

economy
  agriculture industry, 80–84
  Great Depression, 48
  gross state product, **87**
  lumber industry, 84, 86
  manufacturing industry, 79
  mining industry, 84, **84,** 86
education, 64, 82, 89
employment, 79, **80**
endangered species, 17–21
environmental concerns, 17–21,
  22, 24, 26–27, 53
explorers, 36–37

farming, 23–24, 47, 80–84, 85
festivals and fairs, 62–63, 113,
  115–116, 118–119
fish hatcheries, 84
Ford, Gerald, 51
forests, 16, 22, 94
Fort Boise, 40

Fort Hall, 38, 40
Fort Hall Reservation, 44
Frank Church River of No Return
  Wilderness, 22
fur trade, 37–38

geography
  borders and boundaries, 9, 11
  facts, 107
  landscape, 11–12
  mountain ranges, 11–12
  panhandle, 56
  rivers, 11, 12, 14
ghost towns, 97, **97**
gold discovery, 41
golf, 91
Gospel Hump Wilderness, 22
government
  executive branch, 69–70, 72
  judicial branch, 73
  legislative branch, 73
  Native American rights, 74, 77
  state capitol building, 94
Grand Tetons, 12, 101, **101**
Grant, Ulysses S., 77
gray wolf, 20–21, **21**
Great Depression, 48
ground squirrels, **19,** 19–20
Guthrie, A. B., 61

Hagerman Fossil Beds, 98
Hells Canyon, 12, 93, **93**
Hells Canyon National Recreation
  Area, 93
"Here We Have Idaho" (song),
  106
Hispanic population, 59–60
hot springs, 94, 101, 103, **103**
hydroelectric power, 24

Idaho Annual Spud Day, 63

Idaho City, Idaho, 97
Idaho Falls, Idaho, 23, 67
Idaho National Laboratory (INL), 50, 79
Idaho Shakespeare Festival, 63
Idaho Territory, 41, 44–45
Idaho Wildlife Federation (IWF), 18
irrigation, **23,** 23–24

Japanese Americans, 49
Joseph (Nez Perce chief), 45, **45**

King Hill, Idaho, 67
Kutenai war, 51

labor unions, 46–47
Lake Coeur d'Alene, **76,** 77
lakes, 14
Lava Hot Springs, 101
Lewis, Meriwether, **36,** 36–37, 94
Lewiston, Idaho, 44, 93
Lionel Hampton Jazz Festival, 63
livestock, 84
Lochsa River, 14, 94
Lolo Pass, 94
Looking Glass band (Nez Perce), **31**
Lost River Range, 12
lumber industry, 47, **47,** 53, 84, **86**
Lumberjack Days, 62

Macfarlane's four-o'clock, **18**
manufacturing industry, 79
maps and charts
  attractions, **92**
  county, **75**
  employment/workforce, **80**
  ethnic diversity, **58**
  government, **72**
  gross state product, **87**
  land and water, **10**
  population density, **65**
  population growth, **46**
  resources, **85**
  state population, **96**
  ten largest cities, **96**
Massacre Rocks State Park, 62
McCall Winter Carnival, 66, **66**

Meridian, Idaho, 23
Minidoka Relocation Center, 49, **49**
mining industry, 46–47, 53, 84, 91
missionaries, 38–39, 62
Mormons, 40, 56
Mount Borah, 12
Mountain Man Rendezvous, 62
mountain men, 37–38
mountain ranges, 11–12

Nampa, Idaho, 23, 67
National Oldtime Fiddlers' Contest, 62–63
National Wild and Scenic River, 94
Native Americans
  ancient ancestors, 29
  Chief Joseph, 45, **45**
  Coeur d'Alene, 38–39
  cultural celebrations, 59
  European diseases, 44
  firearms, 34
  Great Basin peoples, 33–34, 35
  horses, 32, **32,** 34
  Idaho tribes, 29–30
  Kutenai war, 51
  missionaries, 38–39
  Nez Perce, **31,** 34, 37, 44–45, 53
  Northern Paiute, 33
  petroglyphs, 93
  plateau peoples, 30–32
  population, 59
  powwows, **34**
  rendezvous, 34
  reservations, 44, 45, 59, 74, 77
  rights, 74, 77
  Shoshone, 35
  Shoshone-Bannock, **33,** 33–34, 44
natural resources, 85
nematodes, potato cyst, 82
Nez Perce National Historical Park and Museum, 93
nicknames, 86
nitrogen plant, **78**
North West Company, 37
northern Idaho, 91, 93
nuclear power, 50

Office of Species Conservation (OSC), 19–20
Oregon Territory, 40
Oregon Trail, 39–40, 103
Otter, C. L. "Butch," 70, **71**
Oven-Roasted Jo-Jos (recipe), 83, **83**

panhandle, 91
peregrine falcon, **109**
petroglyphs, 93
pioneers, 39–40
plant life, 16, 17, 18, 108
Pocatello, Idaho, 23
pollution, 26–27
population
  density, **65,** 67
  ethnic diversity, 57–61, **58**
  growth, **46,** 57, 64
  Hispanic, 59–60
  Native American, 59
  per square mile, 23
  state, 57, **96**
  ten largest cities, **96**
potatoes, 47, 80–83, **81**
prejudice, 51, 60–61

racism, 51, 60–61
recreation, 61–64, 89, 93
religion, 56
Riggins, Idaho, 93
River of No Return, 11, **11,** 93
rivers, 11, 12, 14, 23
rodeos, 62, **62**
Ruby Ridge, 52–53

Sacajawea, **28, 36**
Sacred Heart Mission, 39
Saint Joseph's Mission, 93
salmon, 24, 26, **26**
Salmon River, 11, **11,** 14, 24, 93
Salt Lake City, Utah, 56
Sawtooth Mountains, **8,** 12
Sawtooth Wilderness, 22
Selkirk Range, 12
Selway River, 14
Selway-Bitterroot Wilderness, 22
settlers, 39–40
Seven Devils Mountains, 12
Shoshone Falls, 98, **99**

Sierra Silver Mine, 91
Silver City, 97
Silver Valley, 91
Snake River, 12, 23, 24, 53, 98, **99**
Snake River Birds of Prey Natural
    Area, 17
Snake River Plain, 12, **13,** 23, 39
snow and snow melt, 14, **14**
Soda Springs, 103, **103**
southern Idaho, 94, 96–98,
    100–103
Spalding, Henry and Eliza, 38
Spokane, Washington, 56
sport fishing, **88,** 89
state symbols, 104–105

statehood, 45–46
Steunenberg, Frank, 47
Stewart, Tony, 51
Sun Valley, 49, **49,** 100
Sun Valley Summer Symphony, 63

technology industry, 53, 79
Teton, Randy'L, **28**
tourism, 87, 89
trade, 37–38, 87, 89, 93
trading posts, 37, 38, 40
trout fishing, **88**

U.S. Army Corps of Engineers, 24
unions, 46–47

United Kingdom, 87
universities and colleges, 64

Wallace, Idaho, 91
waterfalls, 98, **99**
"Way Out in Idaho" (song), 42–43
weather, 13–15
Weaver, Randy, **52,** 52–53
white supremacists, 51, 60–61
wilderness areas, 17, 22, 98
wildfires, 15, **15**
wildlife, 16–17, 18–21, 108
World War II, 49
Wyeth, Nathaniel, 38

## ABOUT THE AUTHOR

Rebecca Stefoff has written dozens of books for young readers, including *Oregon*, *Washington*, and *Alaska* for the Celebrate the States series. Stefoff grew up in the Midwest, lived for a while on the East Coast, and now lives on the West Coast, not far from the end of the Oregon Trail. She enjoys reading and writing about the geography, exploration, and history of the American West. Her adventures in Idaho while gathering information for this book included white-water rafting on the Salmon River, camping in the Bitterroot Mountains, visiting the Winter Carnival in McCall, sightseeing in Boise, and exploring the historical sites and natural wonders of southern Idaho.